Prologue

I NEVER INTENDED TO go to counselling school and become a therapist. I loved my job working as an Occupational Therapist working in rehabilitation with folks who have physical disabilities. But life happened. One graduate course taken for interest started the slippery slope to getting a full degree in Marriage and Family Therapy.

I graduated with a ton of head knowledge. I had read 1000s of pages and written hundreds more. I scoured the books of models and approaches. However, I don't think I had a complete grasp of what it looked like to sit with a client. When a client, stuck in a posture of pain, came for therapy, what did it look like to respectfully hold space in a way that invited them to be in a healthier place? It petrified me to start my private practice: Did I know enough to actually help people.

Turns out I didn't. Not really, anyway.

It's rather like learning to ride a bicycle. You can watch videos and understand the concepts, but you must get on the bike and sense what it's like to balance on two wheels, enjoy the wind in your hair and manage turns and know when and how to brake. Even once you figure basic cycling out, it's only by being out there that a person can understand what it is to cycle in the rain, or off-road, over curbs and cracks, and in the mud or snow.

You really can only learn by doing it.

That's where my clients come in. I don't know if they knew how much they taught me about being alive, about therapy, and about relationships. They taught me how to be a therapist. Clients came week after week, client after client. When they came back, they told me what had mattered the week before. They advised me what I got right, and they let me know when I got it wrong!

It was humbling, but I am grateful for it all.

I was the expert of the process; those models of therapy and strategies of communication are useful! My clients were the experts of their story. They knew the truth of their experience. They discovered what happened when they tried something different. Together, we collaborated and co-created outcomes that neither of us would have figured out on our own. I discovered a richness to a calling I didn't even know I had.

So much of what clients taught me was paradoxical. Actually, they didn't "teach" me. The most important lessons in life, I think, are better *caught* than *taught*. So much of what I learned was counterintuitive to conventional relationship wisdom. Together, we learned the way to real relationships was messiness, mistakes, and discomfort. We noticed the route to acceptance was authenticity, that tears make life better, and that raw courage is often about tender things like saying, "I'm sorry" and "I love you".

And so much more. So much more.

Wired for Connection

The counterintuitive lessons a therapist learned from her clients

Carolyn Klassen

Wired for Connection

Book Cover by Carolyn Klassen/Zack Ingles

1st edition 2023

To clients, who, in addition to being clients, were unawares
also my teacher
I am grateful for your courage, rawness, humility, candor
and vulnerability.
We shared in what it means to be human,
wired for connection, together

Contents

I didn't know how I could continue being a therapist after my husband left me in 2005. How was I supposed to help others put their lives together when mine has fallen apart? My clients will never know how being with them was healing and restorative. I'd watched them deal with crushing disappointment and abject abandonment and I knew that if they made it through, I would too. Their ability to find their way through their tragedies had me know I would make it through mine.

Their hope and recovery were, at times, ahead of mine. I knew redemption and recovery in my bones because of therapy conversations—so I was OK even when I wasn't OK.

When I had the opportunity to ruin my career every week on live radio, once again, my clients taught me how to do terrifying things. The commitment my clients had to the hard work to show up in their lives challenged me to show up in mine.

When a second chance at love came my way, a client said to me in a loud declarative voice: "Falling in love is terrifying!" I agreed with him with every fibre of my being. Once again, watching my clients live their lives helped me live mine.

Truth is, while I was being their therapist, they were being my teachers. Every one of them. So were my kids, my friends, my now-husband. Having a front-row seat to people as they talk about their lives has helped me stop being a spectator of my own. The life lessons that I've learned with and from clients taught me how to be a stepparent, how to repair the rupture after a disagreement with my now-husband, and so much more.

William Paul Young says: "I suppose that since most of our hurts come through relationships, so will our healing". This line is fundamental to who I am and what I do. And I think it's beautiful and I've experienced it to be true.

I spend my life with people as they sort through their hurts to create the possibility of healing. Little do they know I am learning and growing and healing right alongside them.

The lessons I caught happened in the stories they told, but also in the profound and real interactions I have had in the therapy office. Clients show up to struggle in session. I show up as a companion to struggle right alongside—a fellow journey person. Their trust in me allowed me to see the inside workings of relationships—the beautiful, painful, messy, intricate dynamics that sustain a human being.

Relationships are hard—but we are wired for them. We are wired for struggle and growth. Watching people struggle with their own lives has inspired me to struggle and grow in mine.

Relationships are hard for us all. But if we show up to connect, and we do it anything like right, we learn from each other. We learn from each other in ways that surprise and delight us.

We are wired for connection. I believe that to the core of my being—and conversation with clients has proven it over and over and over.

Often, as we develop relationship literacy, the simple lessons that we were taught as children turn out to differ greatly from the nuanced, more subtle ways of being effective in relationships.

These are our lessons. These are our stories.

I used to think people would only like me if I impressed them. Now I've grown into believing people celebrate me for who I am.

WIRED FOR CONNECTION

Connection, The TEDx talk

I used to think people would only like me if I impressed them. Now I've grown into believing people celebrate me for who I am.

On January 12, 2018, I received an email from an old friend, Mary Anne, who was on the speaker's committee at TEDx Winnipeg. She wrote: "I volunteered to nudge you to apply to be a speaker for this year's event on June 13".

TEDx is a grassroots initiative to "share ideas worth spreading" in local venues. I'm a true dyed-in-the-wool geek at all things TED and TEDx. I had applied and attended local TEDx events and loved them—and admired the speakers. Because of a TED talk, I tie my shoes differently. I stand differently before I speak in public because of Amy Cuddy's TED talk. Susan Cain, in her TED talk, gave me permission to be an introvert. The talk on emotional agility by Susan David is something I made my family watch too. Brene Brown's TEDx talk woke me up to new language that confirmed all the work I had been doing. TED has shaped my life.

The email to invite me to apply to speak at a TEDx event both terrified and thrilled me. It was a fantasy of mine to one day be on a TEDx stage. Note that I say fantasy. It wasn't a plan or even a dream. It was pure delightful fiction in my heart.

I replied:

> Wow. Gulp. Waaaay cool. I would suspect that most people who do any level of public speaking throw the idea around in their brains about speaking at TEDx. I certainly have–but have never seriously considered it—because, well, you know–smart folks should apply—not me! ☺
>
> If nothing else, you have absolutely made my month by sending me this email to contemplate it. I opened the application when I saw they came out just for fun, but it went no further. By suggesting this to me, you have profoundly affirmed me in ways that are significant. Thanx so much.

You can see in my response: I doubted my ability to contribute on the TEDx platform. I questioned my voice. My first inclination is likely similar to what yours has been in situations that intimidate you: "Who, me? No, I couldn't. You will find someone much better." Which is code for: "Me? Stick my neck out that far? 'Put myself out there' in ways that I can get rejected? No thanks. Let me play it safe."

But Mary Anne encouraged me to give it a shot. After a few emails back and forth, I ended our conversation with: "Thanx. You give life wherever you go, y'know?"

Encouragement is fuel for the soul, for us all. Building each other up through a suggestion like this allows others to know you believe in them. We all need to know that people believe in us.

I applied, with the comfort that if the committee didn't believe I could do it, or if my idea wasn't adequate, they wouldn't accept me, and I'd be off the hook. I wasn't sure what I wanted after I applied: to be rejected, which would be disappointing but safe, *or* to be accepted and launch into a terrifying and exhilarating adventure with an organization that I admired and loved.

Frankly, relief through rejection seemed preferable to the terror of being accepted as a TEDx speaker.

I was accepted.

My belly was like Grinch's heart—except worse. The knot in the pit of my stomach grew not 2, but 10 sizes that day. What had I signed up for?

My body felt the pull of what most of us feel when we are intimidated, overwhelmed, or feeling inadequate. I wanted to run and hide. I over thought about what to wear to the first meeting. Before I started, I contemplated quitting.

I noticed my body, as I was preparing to talk about connection, scream at me: "Disconnect! Pull away. Withdraw!"

So often, the desire for connection competes with the desire to disconnect, doesn't it?

I anticipated the opening meeting for speakers for the 2018 TEDx Winnipeg event with terror. I was about to walk into a room with TEDx organizers and speaker coaches and those accepted to speak at a TEDx event. Read: these would be brilliant people who were going to quickly realize I was an imposter.

I was frantic. Was I good enough? Could I do it? I'm a mere mortal. Maybe this was beyond me and only for those who are superhuman.

I did what I always do when I feel out of my league: I armed myself with information. I bought the book about how to speak like a TED speaker.[1] While it had some great tips for crafting a speech to be impactful and exceptional advice for preparing to give an important talk, my most valuable takeaway wasn't for my head—it was for my spirit. The story of Monica Lewinsky, who gave a talk on bullying really struck home. She says, "Nervous is too mild a word to describe how I felt. More like...Gutted with trepidation. Bolts of fear. Electric anxiety.... Plagued by a deep insecurity I didn't belong on the TED stage."[2]

She described no less than 11 specific and distinct anxiety/stress management strategies that she used before her talk.

Her self-doubt was profound: "The night before the speech content rehearsal, three weeks before the conference, I broke down in tears, exasperated that the content was just not gelling. I planned to bow out after the rehearsal but I was shocked by the positive reception. I kept waiting for the *However*...and *But*. They never came."[3]

I had seen Monica's TED talk long before I read about the book. (Have I mentioned I'm a TED geek?) Her talk was professional, proficient, and compelling. I could not see her shaking knees. Ms. Lewinsky looked fabulous. She appeared confident.

I would never have guessed she struggled so much with her own fears prior to and during her TED talk.

Funny how often we measure our insides to other people's outsides and find ourselves falling short, isn't it?

The morning of the first TEDx speakers' meeting, I examined my throat for a tickle that was sure to turn into full blown pneumonia. Nothing. No legitimate reason to back out. And I remembered the courage of my clients to do the hard things in their lives.

And I went to the initial speaker's meeting arm-in-arm, in my mind's eye, with all the clients I know who have done hard things:

- The woman who gave herself permission to stop attending mandatory family gatherings where the uncle who sexually abused her as a child sits across the room.

- A husband who dares tell his wife that he doesn't initiate sex because he isn't confident his performance will measure up.

- The husband who acknowledges he acquiesces in most arguments because he fears rejection.

- An employee who asks her manager for pay equity with her male counterparts.

- The young woman who introduces her female partner to her non-inclusive parents

When clients give me the gift to walk alongside while they are brave in their own stories, I do not walk alone into my own hard experiences.

I was very early for the meeting—again, a symptom of my anxiety. But the assigned meeting room was locked, and as the leaders scrambled to find a room we could access, I chatted with the other speakers.

To my surprise, while they were fascinating people, they were also very ordinary. We talked about where we had parked and how hard it was to find the assigned room. One had recently been on vacation, and we heard about their trip.

I knew I could be there. I could connect with these people.

The opening line of Kerry Stevenson, the chair of the speaker's committee, was this: "Don't be afraid to be afraid."

I wrote that down in big letters.

He told us it's ok to be scared. It's normal to be intimidated. He was clear that we would not be alone. He promised the TEDx volunteers would help us get through this experience. There would be speaker coaches that would provide us with help with each step: brainstorming, writing, editing, fact checking, and on-stage rehearsal. They, too, understood the value of human connection and I was not alone.

The TEDx Winnipeg organization lived out the very values I was planning to extol onstage.

It was still terrifying, but now it was do-able. They connected me with people who understood how to help me.

I can do hard things when I am connected to others.

I started my TEDx Talk[4]:

> *When I went to California for graduate studies in marriage and family therapy, I couldn't have imagined that my most powerful lesson on relationships wouldn't be in the classroom, but in a forest.*

> *On weekends off from studying, I would travel around the state to see its beauty. My favorite and most memorable visit was to the King's Canyon National Park, where I saw some of the largest living organisms on the planet: sequoias trees. These majestic trees can grow more than 80 meters high—that's roughly as high as a 24-story building—and be as wide as 10 meters in diameter. These monstrous trees are able to withstand the roughest weather, and some have done so for more than 2000 years.*

My family and I walked around in hallowed reverence on the pathways around these trees. We were in awe of their enormity. It is a sacred experience to connect with these trees.

The sequoia trees defy description. Pictures don't do them justice. Seriously. A family of four stretched out holding hands around a large one may get only about a third of the way around the tree. A hollowed-out tunnel through the fallen trunk of one sequoia allows cars to drive through. A tree with a hollowed-out base allowed our entire group of 6 to stand inside the tree to pose for a photo—with plenty of room to spare. These trees create their own weather at the top of their canopy.

Incredibly, the roots of sequoia trees go down into the ground only about a half to one and a half meters. It would seem impossible—and yet, is obviously, and remarkably, possible for them to remain standing.

But here's the thing: a giant sequoia never grows alone. It always, ***always*** *grows in a grove. A sequoia weaves its roots in and amongst the roots of other sequoias over time, covering as much as an acre—to create incredible stability. And then these trees actually connect their roots to each other—joining together—so they can help each other out.*

A key to the sequoia trees' survival is their interconnectedness.

Sequoia trees need each other.

They are wired for connection.

Throughout nature, the value of connection is easily seen. I love the idea that a tree that is thirsty at one end of the forest will get water from a tree closer to a water source. They literally hold each other up.

The TEDx talk went on:

> *People are no different. We are wired for connection—we need each other to survive and thrive. We were meant to grow in a forest of humanity; to have lives around us intertwining with ours. People enjoying each other in the everydayness of life and are also ready and steady when circumstances threaten to bend us, ensuring we don't topple over completely in the inevitable storms of life.*

You can then imagine how hard the COVID-19 pandemic was on all of us—when the very thing that we need during times of stress is distress is connection—we were cut off from each other. The very thing that we were doing to slow the spread of the virus was also cutting us off from an essential need in our lives.

What we were doing to stop the spread was also stopping the flow of connection in our lives—something that is as essential to our well-being as food, water, and oxygen.

The TEDx talk continued:

> *Research has found that women with breast cancer with a large network of friends were four*

times more likely to survive as women who were not as connected.

Swedish research found that those with extensive social networks have a lower rate of dementia.

John Cacioppo and his colleagues found that when people had active social lives, they recovered faster after illness.

Julianne Holt-Lunstad's analysis of 148 studies found that people that have better social connections have a 50% reduced risk of early death. The risk of social isolation is comparable to smoking 15 cigarettes a day and carries more risk than obesity or air pollution.

Dr. Holt-Lundstad and her team have studied the impact of relationships on maintaining good health and avoiding ill health. She advocates for people to take the investment in relationships just as seriously as we make other health choices, such as going to the gym or smoking cessation. Her research says that the extent to which people are socially connected will influence rates of heart attack, stroke, Type 2 diabetes dementia and Alzheimer's disease.[5]

Dr. Holt-Lundstad says that hundreds of studies have replicated these findings. Now science can definitively say

"There is scientific evidence that having more and better relationships significantly predicts living longer, while having fewer and poorer quality relationships predicts early death, from all causes." She now advocates for graphic posters around health and well-being to join the posters in the doctor's office that give messages about smoking cessation, and healthy diet. It would be equally or more important to have posters that say: "invest in friends" and "make your relationships meaningful" as a cue to patients to invest in health.[6]

With knees still knocking, but moving to the part of the stage that my speaker coaches helped me decide was the place to remind me of these lines, I said,

> *Strong bonds help cardiovascular health, strengthen immune response, keep brains sharp, and slows cellular aging.*

> *Relationships are an integral part of mental health.*

> *Robert Waldinger, the current head of Harvard Study of Adult Development, says that the clearest and most conclusive message that we get from this 80-year study is that: "Good relationships keep us happier and healthier. Period."*

The Harvard Study of Adult Development began in 1939, following 268 Caucasian men, all 19 years old, when the study began. The study has followed them via questionnaire, extensive interviews, and health documentation throughout their lives, gathering information on health and over all wellbeing. Eventually, researchers added 468 Caucasian men from the neighbourhoods of Boston to the study to create socioeconomic diversity.[7]

The study now extends to include their children—male and female.

Researchers have analyzed hundreds of thousands of documents looking at health risks and social factors which influence longevity and quality of life. The researchers discovered that the most important predictive of a healthy and happy octogenarian was the level of satisfaction with their relationships when they were 50.

Here's the deal: Simply having human beings around you that talk to you and with you regularly is not enough. Meaningful relationships are needed to add years and quality to one's life. Waldinger says: "it's not just the number of friends you have, and it's not whether or not you're in a committed relationship, but **it's the quality of your close relationships that matters**."[8]

So, we are wired for connection, to be sure. But perhaps the more accurate language is, "We are wired for **good** connection". Perhaps that's a given.

Electrical wiring doesn't work when the wires are exposed or brittle or not the right size for the voltage they are to carry. The wiring doesn't work if the wires aren't connected correctly. "White to white, and black to black" is a mantra of a friend who is a very amateur electrician. Electricians spend years knowing how to make those connections effective and safe.

Electricians carefully work to create effective connections that light up a home, a world, our lives.

Why should relationships be any different?

The TEDx team invested in me—they were generous with their time and talents. They showed up to help me be successful. And I showed up for them. I had my TEDx talk recorded on my iPhone and I listened to it on repeat for weeks to do right by their investment in me.

They gifted me the opportunity to tell the world about how significant relationships are. So often, when clients come in with an issue that seems to be about a decision, a situation, a problem, doesn't seem like it's about relationships. Rather, it seems like it's about:

- Should I apply to medical school?
- I'm so depressed I'm worried I won't be able to get to work if it gets any worse
- I'm new to the city and I'm anxious

When we dig deeper, it's about connection:

- The potential medical school student is feeling pressure from their parents—they don't want to disappoint, but they want to be a chef. It's a relationship issue.
- The person who is depressed is mourning the loss of a breakup, and the abortion she had several months ago—the due date of the child if she had chosen to proceed would be next week. It's a relationship issue.

- The person who is starting a new job in a new city is feeling lost without his supportive community around him. He is lonely, and it is translating into anxiety. This is a relationship issue

It might not look like it's about connection with self or others—but as we look "under the hood" of the problem, it comes down to our deep need for relationships—and thus, our great pain when there are relationship stressors.

The organizers of the TEDx event held a BBQ on the evening of the TEDx event. We gathered in Kerry's backyard and ate hamburgers and hotdogs. We high-fived each other and remembered the moments of the day together. By now, the TEDx speakers and TEDx committee volunteers were old friends. We celebrated the connections that night we had forged over the last months. After the months of rehearsals, editing, practicing, memorizing, adjusting, and learning, that evening–we just enjoyed each other.

My participation in TEDx Winnipeg 2018 was an exercise in experiencing everything I said in my TEDx talk. It started with the email that encouraged me to try, and then continued throughout. My coaches, Caity and Stephen, were candid in their feedback to help me be successful. It wasn't always easy, but I knew it was well intentioned—and I am grateful.

I was nervous that day—but I was prepared. My husband, Jim, and our son and some of my friends heard it—a lot–as I practiced.

I was the last of all the speakers. I was more than a little jealous of the speakers who finished before me. One by one, they emerged off the stage, jubilant—and we celebrated! My parents and my friends were in the audience that day, and my coaches were off to the side backstage. They were rooting for me. They believed in me.

We took a group picture of all of us at start of the day—I was part of a team. I was on the stage that day, buoyed by the support of family, friends, and the TEDx team. We did it together. I could it because they believed in me.

"...it's time to prioritize our relationships like our life depends on it. Because it does." **Julieann Holt Lundstad**

I used to think that friendships were good fun and added a little spice to life. Now I know they are an essential food group that literally keeps us alive.

Wired for Connection

Meaningful connections matter

I used to think that friendships were good fun and added a little spice to life. Now I know they are an essential food group that literally keeps us alive.

THURSDAY IS COMING THIS week, as it always does. I will meet with Mary for coffee as she and I have done virtually every week at that time for about 13 years now.

We started when her work colleague—my husband – left us. She called me up as we both felt lost and confused when this man, who was so important to both of us, albeit in different ways, stopped being part of our lives.

We *started* meeting out of crisis. We *continued* meeting because of, well—life.

Coffee on Thursday will mostly be very ordinary. We spent years talking about her mother in a personal care home, and my kids as I single parented them. There was another set of eyes on the challenges when we shared our stories. We have talked about our work, our current stressors and great longing dreams.

In the early years, I ordered a plain tea because I couldn't afford a latte—in recent years, a Starbucks latte is one of my weekly treats. Recently, we have joined a gym, and after our weekly "Stretch and strength" class, we go to their café for our visit and beverage.

We now talk about our mostly mundane lives over for about an hour and a half or so, then embrace each other, and continue about the day. We will most likely not see, talk, or even text each other for a week before we meet again next Thursday.

Occasionally, one of us needs to cancel because of a workshop or a vacation. Once, while she went on a sabbatical, we stopped—but then resumed once her regular rhythms restarted.

If neither of us has specifically cancelled because of an event, I show up. And so does she. We don't arrange it—we just know it's happening.

We show up—our lives connected meaningfully through the slow and real growth that happens as our lives intersect regularly over a very long time. Our roots have grown intertwined in intricate and meaningful ways. I know how she has grown and can celebrate that she no longer worries about things that used to keep her up at night. I can celebrate that in the way that a newer friend cannot.

There is a trust and depth in our conversation. Mary has a right to challenge me the way no one else in the world can—and she does. If she asks me about my part in a mess, perhaps in a parenting moment handled poorly—I answer. She isn't cruel in her challenge—I can tell she loves me when she says something like, "Yikes, that child of yours is driving you crazy. It's hard not to lose it, huh? But I can hear you want to go back to that relationship differently. Let's figure that out."

You can see that her compassionate response isn't indulgent–she doesn't let me off the hook. There is no, "There, there, sweet pet. Of course, you can be pissed off and stay that way. He deserves it." That wouldn't be truly kind to me. She is good for me.

We are there for each other each week. When something hard and lonely comes up, we have a time scheduled—and it **will** get talked about.

Because—Thursday.

During the pandemic, it was one routine that never wavered. We switched to video, her conversation from her bed, and me in mine. We kept meeting—mostly because it didn't occur to us to stop. When people were tired and "zoomed out", we were too! But we never contemplated not meeting.

Turns out those unrelenting Thursday visits became important when Mary's husband was hospitalized with a life-threatening illness—and then got hospital acquired COVID-19. Mary was alone, at home, and floundering with the possibility of losing her life's partner for decades.

She was pulling away and pulling back from most everything—but Thursday mornings are such a routine for us. She kept showing up. During a pandemic and family illness, when connecting with others was almost impossible for her, we kept meeting. When getting together with anybody was hard, the routine of it made our conversations easy.

She loves me, and I love her with the fierce love that grows organically over the years of ongoing authentic and genuine conversation.

Mary, and our conversations, are one of the exceptional gifts of my life.

She has inspired, comforted, cajoled, prayed, and laughed me into being a better version of me. I wouldn't be the same person without those regular and consistent conversations. She continually notices and celebrates the best parts of me—and those parts grow with her showers of love. I am grateful. Mary makes my life better.

In forest language, we are old growth friends. Our lives are deeply interconnected and intertwined at the roots in a manner that isn't visible to anybody who also isn't at the coffee shop on all those Thursday mornings. She provides stability that makes growth possible in my life. I like to think I do the same for her.

In some of the talks I give to various organizations, I speak about my relationship with Mary and its importance in my life. I remember one workshop when a woman said, under her breath, "We could all use a Mary."

Truth bomb, right there.

We all need a Mary.

Johann Hari was a speaker at a conference I attended a few years ago. It was a conference focused on addictions and addiction treatment. He is a journalist who has done a thorough analysis into all matters of addictions. He has examined the research and arrived at the conclusion that: "The opposite of addiction isn't abstinence; the opposite of addiction is connection".[9]

At the conference, Hari spoke of a study in which the researchers asked individuals how many people they had in their lives that they could count on in a time of need. When the study was done in the 1980's, the most common answer was 3.

In 2004, when the study was repeated, he said, the most common answer people give when naming how many people they could call upon as a confidant: zero.

I'll admit it: I was smug hearing this. I thought to myself, "Well, he just said he is quoting American statistics. He is British, and he doesn't properly understand that Canada is different from the United States. We are friendlier, kinder, and better connected."

A person can think a lot in just a few moments. I got shown up when his very next sentence went something like, "And lest you think that I am quoting American stats and this isn't relevant to you, I might let you know this: The only countries that had lower numbers of meaningful connections that the United States were Canada and Iceland."

Ooof. Right in the gut. Twisted the knife.

We are a lonely people.

And things have only gotten tougher since 2004.

In 2012, there was a change in our world.[10] The number of teens with anxiety and depression concerns started increasing at a rate we hadn't seen before.

What is significant to the year 2012?

This is the year where the momentum of technology shifted. It was the first time in history that more people than not had a smart phone. A little computer that fit into a pocket that could connect a person instantly to more information and more people than ever before.[11]

Technology ramped up the speed at which we became more anxious and lonelier and depressed. I think it's time we wrap our heads around the unintended result of having all this ability at our fingertips: technology atrophies the roots of genuine relationships in our lives.

Meaningful relationships are becoming an endangered way of life. In this age of social media, which allows us to instantly connect with anything or anyone with a device that fits in our pocket, we are lonelier than ever. Many have hundreds of friends on Facebook, thousands of contacts on LinkedIn, and will brush up against dozens of people in the day.

And yet, there is pervasive isolation. Roots are going down and out, but not intertwining in the way that only authentic face-to-face encounters nurture and develop. Face-to-face encounters that can only develop by investing hundreds of hours.

In this age of transience, moving away to school, and then moving again once or twice for a career, you may not live near anyone you knew even 5 years ago. The roots that once tangled with others atrophy and wither from inattention.

Life is busy, maybe family and the challenge of a new environment inhibits new relationships of significance developing. Carpools, arranging play dates, checking emails—the administrivia of our lives has our schedules so full, there is no time for relationship root development. And in the middle of a full life with hundreds of contacts daily, the only answer to "How are you?" is the polite and noncommittal social courtesy of "fine".

In a world that is laser focused on images and brief video of snapchat and Tik Tok, we are used to developing instant meaning in the tiniest of sound bites. Which means, perhaps, there is less real development of depth in our relationships.

This is an incredible seismic shift from humanity throughout the rest of history. Even a few generations ago, most would live in the same community for a lifetime, being exposed to the same community of perhaps a couple of hundred people.

Folks would walk a spell to the neighbour's house for a couple of eggs and visit over tea before the return home. Those hours of quiet walking, without earbuds tuned to a podcast, allowed for thoughts to marinate on the way there and clarify the discussion on the way home.

Really, there was so much more opportunity to develop the relationship with oneself before cars, radios, speakers, and earbuds.

A man might go over to help with the birthing of a new foal, sitting at length by lantern-light, with nothing to do but chat about this and that with the neighbour.

There was opportunity to wend the tendrils of their lives around each other through sometimes idle conversation, and sometimes, the pouring out of a heart that only happens when the threshold of safety has developed over hours.

Increasingly, so much of contact is through text and email which misses the eye contact which is so very necessary to develop trust and real kinship with another. We exchange the real face-to-face relationship intertwining of our lives for the expedient but hollow networking through electronic means.

What is instant is also ultimately unsatisfying. What is easy and expedient is also root deadening.

We will transition to new friends as we change jobs, graduate from high school and college, find a life partner with friends they bring into our lives. Novel connections are new energy that will invigorate our lives. Technology is making our lives more informed. (I created my first flower spray last week for a wooden arch, and thanks to Youtube, it turned out great!) However, even as new roots extend to new relationships, and we use instant technology to connect with people from around the world), old growth friendships are essential to our well-being.

Just as conservationists protect the sequoia roots, and fight to prevent clear cutting of ancient trees, we need to preserve the old growth forest of friendships in our lives. When relationships have depth and meaning, chopping them down for firewood is a travesty.

The old-growth trees of friendship need careful conservation to maintain the ecology of our souls.

When meaningful relationships help us live longer, it would seem we are not investing enough to create meaningful and rich relationships. For a country obsessed with health, so much so that we are inundated with vitamin pills, fitness apps, gyms to join, diet plans and the like, I wonder if we aren't missing something important when we seek to be healthier: relationships.

Rich and meaningful relationships that last are certainly not always easy, but they are worth it.

"I think if I've learned anything about friendship, it's to hang in, stay connected, fight for them, and let them fight for you. Don't walk away, don't be distracted, don't be too busy or tired, don't take them for granted. Friends are part of the glue that holds life and faith together. " ***Jon Katz***

I used to think that we were
thinking beings that also feel.
Now I know it is far more accurate to
conceptualize that we are feeling
beings that also think.

Wired for Connection

The wiring of connection: feelings are fundamental

I used to think that we were thinking beings that also feel. Now I know it is far more accurate to conceptualize that we are feeling beings that also think.

LAST YEAR, AT A 3-day workshop I facilitated, one participant pronounced on the first evening: "My boss doesn't have any feelings." She described how he doesn't seem to portray much emotion—he is flat in his expression, and just quietly goes about his job. She was noticing the contrast of her manager to another participant (who was herself a manager) in the workshop that was describing her personal response to the challenges her team was facing.

She was caring and thoughtful, and incorporated the feelings of her staff into her decisions.

"I wish my boss had feelings like you do," she said.

As the workshop continued, she spoke about how frustrated she felt at work about some workplace dynamics that were being ignored. She complained about the lack of support she felt when times were challenging—this manager tucked himself away in his office.

By the end of the workshop, she realized he **did** have feelings. The problem lay in in that the feelings he had prevented him from showing up as an effective manager at the workplace. She wasn't sure if his feelings were fear or anxiety or discouragement—or if his disconnection had to do with numbing feeling he was trying to avoid.

If he was a thinking manager without feelings (if that were possible), he would have shown up as an engaged person who actively dealt with problems like unexplained project delays, dealing with absenteeism and tardiness, and so on. The manager's department was falling apart, and he was not addressing the issues.

It wasn't facts that had him avoid addressing the situation.

So, it had to be his feelings.

Jill Bolte Taylor is a neuroanatomist says, "Most of us think of ourselves as thinking creatures that feel, but we are actually feeling beings that think."[12]

There are many that would dispute this statement that neurobiologically, we are foremost *feeling* beings. The uber-logical among us believe they think through decisions and only act on the facts.

Feelings impact behavior all the time as we *feel* emotion:

- Road rage
- Jubilant behavior (or communal anger/devastation) with thousands of others at major league sports games
- The "silent treatment" that can last for days after a fight
- Slow walking a response on a project to the boss

Feelings impact behavior as we choose to *heighten* the bodily feeling of emotion:

- Bungee jumping, roller coasters, hang gliding, scuba diving, race car driving, parachuting
- Horror movies
- Relaxation massages, hot tubs
- That amazing feeling after a hard workout (that some tell me they have—I'm still waiting for it)

Feelings impact behavior as we *avoid/numb* emotion.

- Going to the bar after she breaks up with you, or after he fires you—to drink until you don't feel anything.
- Smoking weed or eating a marijuana gummy to release yourself from the day's stresses.

- Shopping for things you don't need and can't afford because it's been a brutal day.
- Eating your carbohydrate of choice when you've had a fight with your bestie. (BBQ potato chips are my drug of choice.)

Feelings impact behavior in real world ways:

I totalled my car on my way home from a therapy appointment where the therapist challenged me to contemplate the reality that my marriage was going to end, regardless of how much I didn't want it to. True story. To be clear: not on purpose. I did not see the car that T-boned me. I could have sworn it was clear to cross the road.

When I'm feeling great, I get more done. When I'm stressed about an email, I avoid getting it done and generally am less productive. Who of us doesn't put off cleaning the bathroom or sorting out that drawer because we don't like the feeling we get when we think about approaching the task?

Feelings impact relationships.

We avoid a friend who was critical or made us uncomfortable the last time we got together. Further, we avoid the conversation that would say, "I'd rather not avoid you. Can we just talk about how I was offended the last time we got together?" We easily call up the friend who laughs at our stories and is generous with compliments and affirmation.

Don't we all avoid certain conversations with our partners because we are nervous about the outcome or fear judgement? It's so easy to hug people who love us because of the warm feeling we get from the hug, and not so easy to hug the ones who are prickly and stand-offish. We scroll through our photos and share memories on social media because of the love we feel.

Feelings impact health and wellbeing.

The body holds the pain of past trauma, the bitterness and resentment of hurts, and the stress of a current situation.

Emotion affects blood pressure, cardiac health, immunity, gut health, joint pain, and so many other parts of health.

Dr. Marc Brackett is a research psychologist who set up a situation where one set of teachers would be a good mood, and another were set to be in a bad mood. He then asked them all to grade the same paper. There was a full one to two grade difference in the final mark of the paper between the two groups.

The most striking part of this study for me was this: When the researchers asked the teachers about the impact of mood on their evaluation of the paper, 90% of the teachers insisted their internal state it had no impact.[13]

Feelings impact us often beyond our awareness. And in a way we often would want to deny, **our feelings impact others** in real world ways, too.

Imagine: a professor has a fight with his partner before he finishes grading the last few papers—these papers are given a lower grade, and a student falls just shy of getting into a PhD program or failing to get the scholarship necessary to complete a degree.

What I notice in my practice is that the people who think that their feelings aren't underlying every action and decision are dangerous. The lack of self-awareness means that they impose their feelings onto others unbeknownst to anybody—including themselves.

Feelings may be inconvenient, but they are information to our body that we then incorporate into our thoughts and actions. If we are conscious about our feelings, we can then mitigate those responses and make conscious choices about the impact of those feelings.

Simply put, your insistence that feelings do not impact your decisions has you become a marionette with the feelings pulling the strings beyond your awareness.

A huge part of my work as I help people better connect with each other is having people first connect with themselves. As people have a better understanding of their inner world, they are then better able to connect with others.

Sam and Jane have come to therapy to figure out why they have the same fight repeatedly—and when they speak about the latest one, they can't even remember the inciting incident that started this argument. They get along well, are great friends, but get stuck in the loop that can derail them for a couple of days.

As our conversation continues, we literally draw out the pattern on a sheet of paper. Jane gives Sam critical feedback (e.g., You left your cup on the counter again. Please put it in the dishwasher).

Sam gets defensive (e.g., It's only a cup. It's no big deal. Why are you even bringing this up?)

Jane gets louder ("IF ITS NO BIG DEAL THEN JUST DO IT!!"). Sam then leaves the room. Jane then follows him and continues. Sam finds a way to shut a door or go outside to get away from Jane.

This the loop on the "outside"—the view that a movie camera would capture. As a therapist, I look at the view from the inside. What is the internal, unseen dynamics within each person?

We must start somewhere—Sam is up first. With some gentle and tender therapeutic work, we discover that Jane's initial feedback to Sam touches the part of him that feels inadequate for Jane. He resists the idea that he made a mistake because he is worried that she will find him so flawed that she won't love him anymore. So, he pushes back against Jane to prove he is good enough.

I don't decide this for him—we discover it together. He is, however, somewhat surprised that these truths emerge because this is the first time he has slowed down to reflect on this with support. It's difficult for him to acknowledge this because even her knowing this risks judgement from her and, potentially, the loss of her love.

Now Jane is up: Jane feels ignored when Sam walks out of the room. She panics when he walks away. She fears he has rejected her and so she follows him.

I help her look a little at how that feeling of fear that she has at that moment (that she isn't even aware of because of how upset she is) commandeers the situation. He needs some time and her feelings are so powerful she can't notice the larger situation to choose her actions calmly and effectively.

At the end of the session, I suggest we haven't yet addressed the dynamics, we've only just discovered them. I invite them to go into the next incident of "critical feedback" with the full awareness that as they go through the predictable drama, they each do so with full awareness that his defensive response arises out of his fear that he isn't good enough, and her frantic chasing as he goes to cool off arises out of her fear of rejection.

I stress they are NOT to change anything; they are just to note their feelings as they go through the well-worn pattern of argument.

When I do this with a couple, it *always fails*. Always.

Because once they are aware of their feelings, their behavior changes the next time they have the argument. He softens and gets less defensive. She takes a deep breath and if he leaves, waits for 20 minutes before she goes to continue the conversation.

I haven't taught them to do this. I don't need to. When they are more aware of their emotions and how their body is feeling those emotions, they can make choices that are more effective. They avoid a conflict.

We still have work to do in therapy to ensure that the pattern stays changed, but increased awareness of underlying emotion immediately alters the fight they have felt powerless to change.

Awareness of emotion within oneself and in the other affects our ability to connect effectively with others.

The challenge is that to be aware of emotion, we need to have language and understanding of it. Just like we need to know how letters combine to form words which combine to form sentences as part of developing reading literacy, we need to develop a vocabulary of emotions and how we identify the feelings that emotion gives us. Simply, emotional literacy is essential to better understanding ourselves and others.

Emotional literacy is essential to developing better connections.

When Brené Brown and her colleagues surveyed over 7000 people, they found that the average number of emotions participants could identify was 3: happy, sad, and angry.[14] Most of us did not develop emotional literacy at the same pace we develop reading literacy. Let's avoid the blame game about why and how that is—let's just accept this as a reality.[15]

As we develop a better understanding of emotions—the names of emotions, how they feel in our bodies, what context they are created, how they impact us—we can choose how we want to process them internally, and how we want to express them externally. This is a game changer in relationships.

There's even an app for it!

It's not easy to learn something as an adult. But once you start, you'll relationships will thank you.

"Most of us were not taught how to recognize pain, name it, and be with it. Our families and culture believed that the vulnerability that it takes to acknowledge pain was weakness, so we were taught anger, rage, and denial instead. But what we know now is that when we deny our emotion, it owns us. When we own our emotion, we can rebuild and find our way through the pain." **Brené Brown**

I used to think that guilt and shame
were the same.
Now I know that shame is inevitable and
needs to be worked through, but it is
entirely different from guilt—which I want
to be awake to so it can profoundly
influence me in my life.

Guilt and shame

I used to think that guilt and shame were the same. Now I know that shame is inevitable and needs to be worked through, but it is entirely different from guilt—which I want to be awake to so it can profoundly influence me in my life.

As a single mom, I didn't know that my casual-scrolling-with-a-purpose on Thursday, October 21, 2010, would change the direction of my life—as well as countless other people—but it did. I clicked on a link from a friend on Facebook and met Dr. Brené Brown, a shame and vulnerability researcher, on her blog.

The blog she wrote about imperfection and authenticity I found and read that day is no longer on the internet, but my writing about it on Friday, October 22, 2010,[16] still is. I dug deeper into her material. With little difficulty, I must have soon found her 2010 TEDxHouston talk on "The Power of Vulnerability"[17] that went viral, and has north of 19 million viewers on Youtube and 62 million on the TED.com website as of this writing.

As a therapist, I've always known about the power and impact of shame—though I think I confused shame and guilt for a lot of years. Maybe you have, too. I had to read one counselling book per week during a counselling practicum and record the reading in my practicum hours log. My professor wrote a comment one week which has always stuck with me which said something like: "Why all the reading about shame? Maybe time to move onto something else?" And I remember thinking, "Well, shame seems so important in so much of the work I am doing with clients. I need to learn about it!"

So, when I stumbled across Brené Brown's work, it didn't change what I knew to be true about shame as a therapist, but her work sharpened and clarified my understanding and language around shame. My clients have always talked about shame with me. However, once I started hearing and speaking back to them what they had just told me using the language and words that Brené Brown developed, they became animated as people are inclined to do when they feel deeply understood.

I was articulating what they were trying to tell me in a clearer, more focused way. People understood themselves better once I used the vocabulary that Dr. Brown used in her work.

In early December, 2013, I made my way down to San Antonio, Texas, for a week with her organization, for the inaugural The Daring Way™ training. I wanted to better understand the material and how to work with it. My clients found it life changing—and so did I.

Years ago, as I was learning how to understand shame and its effects on me, I went to a Josh Groban concert with Melanie, our client care manager at Conexus Counselling. We are friends as well as colleagues at the counselling clinic. The stage was at one end of the oval of the arena and our seats were not-quite-at-the-other-end of the arena on the side. This meant that when I sat back in my seat, the stage was to my very far right.

The woman sitting to my immediate right was excited to be there. I like Josh Groban—but she was a dyed-in-the-wool Grobanite—to the core. She was passionate in her desire to soak up every precious moment with Josh Groban in the same (albeit large) room as she.

As a result of her desire to get the very best view she could, she leaned forward, leaving me being able to see only the back of her head when I looked at the stage. Now, I may not be a true Grobanite, but if I'm going to be fortunate enough to be at a concert, I'd like a view. Frankly, I can look at the back of a person's head and listen to a CD at home for a lot less hassle and the same effect.

Melanie was sitting to my left, which didn't leave her with a lot to see either. She poked me to poke the Grobanite to my right to ask her to lean back. It seemed an obvious thing to do, right? Except I didn't want to poke the woman. I just didn't want to.

So, I didn't.

Fortunately, within a few minutes, Mr. Groban let me off the hook by coming to the very center of the arena to sing a few songs and my seat mate sat back to enjoy him much closer and more in front of us. I was relieved.

While I was sitting in the dark, listening to the beautiful music and melodic tones of Josh Groban's voice, I reflected on my strange hesitancy. At the time, I stood in front of

50 students regularly and lectured to them for hours. I provided various workshops. I chaired a committee. I knew how to speak up like it was my job—because it was!

I contemplated, "Why would I be so hesitant to just ask a person to sit back in her chair?" It was a question that had me curious. It would seem to take a lot more guts to teach graduate students or go live on radio. What was going on?

What would be my hesitation in tapping her on the shoulder? I let my gut give honest answers: Well, she might scowl at me, and not be happy that I asked her to lean back.

Then another layer of questioning to the response: What would be so awful about her scowling that I dared to ask her that to lean back?

I didn't like the answer that was underneath my answers: I was scared.

I mean, not stark terror, but in a way I hadn't thought about previously, I was fearful of her possible reaction. I dreaded her possible response, because of the fear I would have if she scowled. As I dug down, I found myself realizing I was operating out of a thought that I only found with further curiosity: "If she is nasty to you, it's because you've been a naughty, presumptuous little kid, asking for something that only benefits you. That's shameful and selfish to ask for something like that. You will deserve the look she will give you because you are mean." I felt inadequate, small—not enough.

I realize this doesn't sound logical. To ask a stranger to lean back in her seat isn't a big deal—except I was hooked by the emotion of shame. Shame isn't logical. It is real. And when we aren't aware of it, it hijacks us and takes over. It echoes from some place deep inside, sometimes from years prior.

No wonder I didn't want to tap her on the shoulder to ask her to lean back! Not if I was going to feel scolded from some deep part of me if she should not like my request.

Of course, once I recognized the shame, I could have a further little talk with myself. I reminded myself that a scathing look from her would say more about her than it did about me. I could tell myself that if she was nasty, it may have been because she had a bad day or bad month or bad year, and that she was just grumpy for reasons that didn't have anything to do with me. I could tell myself that she may lack insight into my predicament if she was less than pleasant. And I could tell myself that maybe she wouldn't even react badly—it was just my assumption she would.

Unbeknownst to Mr. Groban, he then gave me a chance to practice. About that time, Mr. Groban moved back to the main stage. Once again, my seat mate tipped all the way forward to enjoy the concert.

It took me a few minutes, but practiced courage as my behavior aligned with my spirit. Bolstered by my own little pep talk, I tapped her on the shoulder. She whipped around, and I briefly mimed and spoke a few words about what I was asking. She immediately apologized and leaned back. Her back was stuck like glue to the chair for the rest of the concert.

It worked! None of what I was fearing, and assumed would happen, happened!

In fact, it had the opposite effect, I think. She didn't look at me for the rest of the concert, even though we had chatted intermittently while we waited for the concert to start. I rather wonder if she felt her own shame for having leaned forward and obscuring my view, even though that wasn't at all my intent.

Shame is such a tricky beast. I can't control or predict or remove another person's shame response, even if I wanted to.

Brené Brown uses this definition of shame: Shame is the intensely painful feeling or experience of believing that we are flawed and therefore, unworthy of love, belonging and connection. It's the feeling of, "I'm not enough".[18]

She describes 3 things to be true about shame:

First, all have it. Everyone who is capable of connection and empathy struggles with shame. Psychology references people who struggle with empathy as having psychopathic or sociopathic tendencies. When I feel like I'm not enough to do something, like a radio or television interview or say, write a book like the one you are holding in your hands, I remember that this feeling of "not enoughness" means I'm not a psychopath.

Knowing that helps me feel better. Weird, but true. It puts a quirky smile on my face, and I get over myself—a little. I'm still feeling the feeling, but it no longer overwhelms me.

Second, it's hard to talk about it. Shame hates being talked about. People don't know how to talk about it. The very feeling of shame has people unwilling to admit the feeling to themselves—and certainly not to others. So often, when I start talking about shame in a group of people, it's like the lightbulb goes on. I'm saying things they have known for years but have never uttered—could never utter. The *knowing was a feeling*, not in words.

We can't talk about it if we are ashamed of shame—which we are—except we don't even realize it. If we don't talk about it, we don't even know how to think about it!

Third, the more we talk about shame, the less control it has over us. I talk about shame wherever I go. *Everywhere* I go. I love leading a workshop or a weekend retreat and watching people feel released from the power of their own shame as they name it, understand it. Their eyes light up and although it's hard to describe, it's rather like they have found greater freedom. They start to make decisions about the feeling of shame, rather than shame making the decisions for them.[19]

Shame influences us in so many ways. Once you know what to look for, you notice how often it pops up in your life in ways that have you get small and pull away, or get defensive and engage in what I call, "huff-puffery"—getting all big and defensive/too loud. You'll notice reactions of others and realize it is likely shame doing the talking.

Once you know about shame, you can't un-know it. It *will* change your life.

We are wired for connection.

This idea isn't just the name of my company, or a cute tagline. It is my life's work.

If connection is as important as food, water, and oxygen to our overall health and wellbeing, then the fear of disconnection is utterly terrifying.

The closeup of the picture of Michelangelo's Creation of Adam is something I have long had above the heads of my clients on the loveseat that they are seated on during therapy sessions with me.

It is important to me as a therapist to have that picture there. My clients have taught me, over and over, that the key to movement in therapy is to understand that each client is wired for connection. When the need to connect is high, the fear of disconnection is also high.

Clients come to me for:

- Mental health issues such as anxiety and depression
- Relationship issues in their marriage, families, friendships, or workplace
- Distress in their job or friendship group or community
- Challenges with everything from dysregulated alcohol use to showing up on time for work, or having too much junk in their house
- Or any other number of things. Every time I think I might have heard it all, someone comes in with another uniquely nuanced and complex scenario in their life

Regardless of the reason for therapy, if we keep peeling back the layers (as I did for myself in the Groban concert) together, we learn of the need for connection and/or the fear of disconnection and how we play into the issue in a significant way.

The fear of being unlovable, the concern of being rejected, or the distress of potentially being abandoned pulls the strings of a person's mental health, relationships, and well-being.

The closeup of the centre of Michelangelo's picture with the two fingers straining to connect with each other in a life-giving way has become so significant to me that it became part of my logo:

Shame—the fear of disconnection—is just as critical in shaping in our lives as our inherent desire and need to connect. It comes up again and again.

Shame and guilt look similar at first blush: they are about feeling bad about self, but they are fundamentally different.

Shame says: "I am bad". It is about me—all of me. Who I am. It labels me in a way that leaves me trapped and stuck. If I am bad, then I am hooped. A bad apple is just, well, bad.

There's nothing to be done. I will always be in shame.

Guilt says: "I did a bad thing". It is about my behavior—what I've done. It gives me options. I can make a different choice. I can recognize when something I've done is out of alignment with my values and who I strive to be, and subsequently decide to do things differently.

It is common to say, "Shame on you". Often, in the media, I hear a commentator hope that a politician or celebrity or CEO feels ashamed of their unethical or otherwise terrible behavior.

I think I'd rather that person feel guilty about it—and change what they are doing.

I spent a decade as a single mom. Those were years of high demands, heavy burdens, unexpected tasks and a pile of things calling my attention. I often felt preoccupied with work, even though my priority is my family.

One day, on my way home from work, I was running a little late, but I dashed into the store because I knew we were short of bread and milk. As full as my brain was with work stuff, I was feeling rather proud that I managed to get what we needed for essentials. If there were two things that are important in my house, it was bread and milk—the stuff of adolescent boys!

I scrambled to do a bit more work in between the cracks of life after work.

There was a game that night. It was a season ending playoff game, and my son's team lost. He was sad, and the car ride home was somber. It was punctuated with proclamations of disappointment over the officiating, frustration with his teammates, and some general disgruntlement, as is common for all boys who hate to lose.

I held my tongue (with difficulty) as he rambled on about the many ways the loss was unfair. It was a high school playoff game—I knew that a year from now, it would be no big deal and all the perceived slights would be forgotten. I also knew that any whisper of this would not be well received on this drive home in the car.

Timing, amiright?

I gritted my teeth to ensure he only heard support and empathy.

I was past exhausted, but I had gotten the necessities done, held my tongue when it was hard, and was ready to collapse when I get home.

We walked in the door, and my son went to make sandwiches for his lunch the next day. He grumbled about the bread I had rushed to purchase on my way home.

The bread is small, according to him.

He says that he will have to make 5 sandwiches in order to have enough to eat.

And I say, "OK, make 5 sandwiches". I say this with some irritation.

He says that making 5 sandwiches is a lot more work than making 2 sandwiches.

I say, "It's the same number of square inches. No big deal." Growing irritation.

He says that the *bread to crust ratio* is all wrong, and he doesn't like crusts and 5 sandwiches have a lot of crust.

It is, at this moment, I go into the kitchen and LOSE IT on him. I tell him many inane things about how it's no big deal, how ungrateful he is, how he should be glad we have bread at all. I accuse him of a crime with the bread—I'm not sure what or why. My volume is much higher than I'm proud of. I probably say a few other things that aren't pleasant or reasonable. I honestly can't remember all I said, but I may have mentioned something about starving children in other parts of the world who would love multiple small sandwiches.

None of this is rational or reasonable.

At one point, this son looks at me and calmly points out that I'm the only one who is yelling.

That does not help.

At some point, I send him to bed and tell him I will make his stupid sandwiches. There is a teeny, tiny part of my brain that understands that I am not rational, and that the best thing is to remove my son from my presence so that I will have less opportunity to inflict damage.

Damage control.

This only looked like an argument about bread size. (And to be fair, the bread was considerably smaller than our usual rye bread)

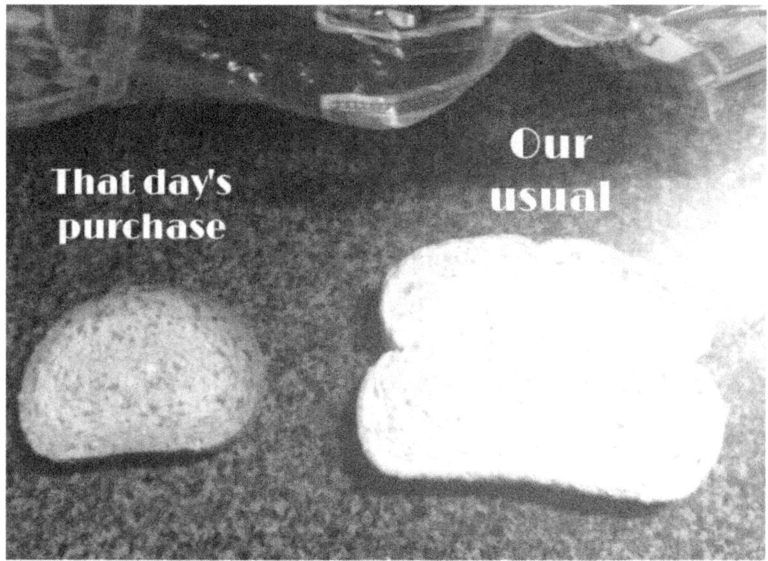

The day I yelled at my JTM, it was about bread size.

I went to bed that night knowing that my son's last contact with a human being for the night was his mother yelling at him. If I hadn't felt like a bad mother before, now I *really knew* I sucked as a mom.

He left for school the next morning early, and I began my day—again, teaching a university class, seeing a few clients, and then zipping home to make supper. But in the back of my mind, I kept mulling about what had happened the night before to make sense of it. I talked with my clients as I looked at the picture of the two fingers reaching and straining to connect to each other. Talk of shame as clients reflected on their situation reminded me of my own.

It was then I realized that my over-the-top outburst at my son was about my shame.

All day long, the previous day, in my busy and preoccupied state, *I'd struggled to maintain my position in the "good mom" category as I felt myself dangerously close to slipping into "bad mom" category.* I'd been hustling for my worthiness by deliberately doing "good mom" things to earn "good mom" status (which never works, but that doesn't stop us from trying, right?). Squeezing in the grocery shopping for essentials and biting my tongue were me hustling to prove my worthiness—that I was "good enough" being a mom. I got to the game despite my exhaustion—because "good moms" go to their kids' games.

As a single mom, I was inevitably struggling with the fear I was slipping into the "bad mom" category. Working two jobs and raising two active sons meant that I felt like I was "never enough".

With the advantage of clients working through their shame, I realized that when my son complained about the bread size, I heard it as a complaint that I was a bad mom. What kind of mom can't even buy bread properly? Answer: bad ones.

In my exhausted, vulnerable state, it seemed to me he was confirming for me what I already had been struggling with and trying to overcome all day: "I am a bad mother". I felt put into the "bad mom" category—and came out swinging.

(Now, I'll just point out the obvious: there is an irony in yelling at one's child to demonstrate that one is a good mother. But shame does that—it pulls us into the very behaviors we seek to avoid.)

It took me the better part of that day to *process my shame and transform it into guilt.*

I want to have **made** a mistake, not **be** a mistake.

By the time we re-connected as a family over supper the next day, I could tell my son, "I try hard to be a good mother. Really hard. Yesterday, it was hard to be a good mother because work was hectic. I worked to squeeze in time to shop for that bread. You were not easy to be around after the loss and I was tired and frazzled. When you criticized the size of the bread slice, **the story I told myself** was that you thought I was a bad mom. Good moms buy the right bread, and because it wasn't the bread you wanted, it meant I was a bad mom. I hate being a bad mom, and I reacted very strongly to being called a bad mom."

Sometimes, kids have a wisdom that is simple, but profound. He just said, calmly: "Mom—it was about the bread. Only about the bread."

"Yeah, now I get that. I'm sorry."

Once I felt guilty about the bread (and my yelling at him) rather than ashamed, I could reconnect with him. I could apologize and we could restore our relationship back to a place of being solid with each other.

I *want* to feel awful when I make mistakes because I *hate* feeling awful. Feeling awful is a powerful motivator—I want to relieve myself of the discomfort by taking care of what I did that created that feeling. Circling back to the conversation with an apology and making it right relieves that "awful" feeling.

As a bonus, *feeling awful* is a powerful teacher—memory of this pain is a welcome reminder to do better next time. I did some brainstorming and talked to another single mom to figure out how to handle difficult moments when I'm tired and feeling inadequate.

Guilt helps make me grow into being a better person in a way that shame can't.

"We cannot grow when we are in shame, and we can't use shame to change ourselves or others."
Brené Brown

I used to think that relationships mostly fell apart when people were mean to each other.
Now I know relationships often fall apart because of shame.

How shame messes up connection

I used to think that relationships mostly fell apart when people were mean to each other. Now I know relationships often fall apart because of shame.

When Jim and I got married, we had 5 children between us, all boys, living at home. While 4 of them were young adults, he did have an 11-year-old. His youngest had so much transition in his young life, we felt the best way for us to move forward as we joined our lives was for me and my kids to move into his house, only about a 5-minute drive from where I had lived prior to our marriage.

I sold my house, and *his* house became *our* house when we wed. We deliberately worked to ensure that it was a house that was mine too—and to that end, we fulfilled a dream I had my entire life. We purchased a hot tub for our backyard. We made quite a sight, I'm sure, as all 7 of us went into hot tub stores and would climb inside the hot tubs to see how we all fit as we made our choice.

We had dreams of bonding this family together with the hot tub.

Turns out that the hot tub didn't need to fit all of us. Jim and I soon found out that if we were in it, the kids were not.

It worked out well though—as newlyweds, it seemed we were forever surrounded by boys and their friends, and girlfriends and all manner of, "Where's my uniform?" "Who ate the leftover pizza?" "Has anybody seen my _____? (Insert any number of things in this blank)"

Jim and I found that a soak in the jetted tub in the evening became a haven of quiet in an otherwise chaotic life. It was a haven where we were "husband and wife" and not preoccupied in our roles as parents.

One Sunday evening in early spring, he and I were discussing plans for the week. He and I both own our own small businesses, and we spoke about the next week. Jim's business is seasonal, and he was just heading into his busy season. I love brainstorming and suggested several ideas for marketing, which he said he liked and would implement the following day.

Monday was a busy day for me—a stressful lecture in the morning at university, and clients all afternoon. Friends of all kinds were coming over Monday evening to watch a basketball game. After supper, before the guests arrived, I was at the stove stirring a pot of chocolatey-syrupy goodness for puffed wheat cake to put out for the party.

It is no surprise that another good time to have a quiet conversation without kids in our chaotic household was when there was any work to be done in the kitchen! It gave

Jim and me a few private moments to catch up on each other's day before the party began. I asked Jim what he had done that day, and he gave me a full itinerary of things he had done—laundry, cleaning, and grocery shopping. The problem was, was that it wasn't what ***we*** had decided he should do when we discussed it. I became terribly (and yes, it was terrible) quiet and he sensed it. I was tired—which is never good for conversations, because any of us are more likely to be sensitive.

He asked me about my silence, and I took a deep breath and let him know that I was disappointed about his choices for that day. I chose my words carefully because I knew that I had the potential to be mean about it, and I worked hard to not be offensive in my words. He looked at me for what seemed forever. Then, he walked out of the kitchen. Silently. He had no words before he left..

Let me emphasize: He turned heel and walked out of the kitchen without speaking.

I was still stirring the pot—puffed wheat cake goo requires 3 minutes of constant stirring while it boils to reach critical temperature so I couldn't follow him from the room. It's safe to say that my stirring had, ahem, more passion to it—more vigour and frequency after he left. It seemed rude that he would abruptly leave mid-conversation, especially since I had been kinder to him than I might have been.

If that sounds smug of me to say, perhaps you'd be accurate. I'm not proud of telling that part of the story, but for completeness, I include it.

I finished making the square. I wiped the bathroom down. I lit some candles—because everyone knows that the NCAA finals are best enjoyed by candlelight! I tidied up, I puttered about for about 45 minutes. Nothing. Nothing from him.

I moved from being tired and annoyed to being angry. It was driving me a little crazy. In my mind, he had asked the question, and when I gave him a candid response that was truthful and real, he pulled away. He was punishing me for being honest. That did not sit well with me.

But here's the thing: 6 days later I was giving a talk in my church on Sunday morning on the topic of—drum roll, please—marriage. In the big picture, integrity is a value that I hold to be important.

In the immediate moment, though, integrity was inconvenient.

I knew I was talking to hundreds of people about being in good relationship in marriage in just a few days. And darn it, if I'm gonna talk about it, I gotta live it. I was upset with him, and if I didn't initiate doing some repair after the rupture, I couldn't speak with integrity.

So, on that Monday I talked to myself: "Carolyn, Jim is not a jerk. He's not actually a guy who punishes you for something you've said, huh? You know that. Maybe stop acting like that's what you know he did. There must be more to this picture."

I had to admit to myself that the guy had been busy with housework all day instead of the agreed upon tasks—which I know to be a formally single mother's dream come true. To be upset about someone doing the laundry seemed off-kilter—even as I was still upset.

To gather my thoughts, I went to light a couple of more candles in the bathroom. I then went into his office. I sat down to say the line that I had composed and then rehearsed a couple of times: "You walked away when I answered you and you've been quiet since. The story I am telling myself is that you are punishing me for answering a question that you asked me."

His mouth dropped open. He was surprised. He responded, "No, Carolyn, I left the kitchen because you were right, and it hurt for me to admit it. I didn't know what to say. And I'm sitting here now doing some of the things that we had decided were important. Today, I did the easy things, not the right thing, and I'm correcting that now."

"Oh."

There wasn't much more to say.

Not sure there was much more to be said. I felt much better. I hope I also expressed some gratitude, but I can't remember.

I can tell you that we went on to have a lovely evening with the tension beautifully resolved. It's much easier to have friends over when there isn't underlying strain!

The next day, Tuesday, we were back in the hot tub in the late evening, and we continued the conversation. Jim, to his credit, was the one who circled back and brought it up again. I think my love for him grew two sizes that day, as I saw him return to where he had made an error. That's not easy to do—and something that most of us avoid.

When he revisited what happened, it told me that I mattered.

He told me that he had spent some of the day digging deeper into the experience. He realized that while I was stirring and noticing that he hadn't done the marketing things as assigned, there was a part of him that jumped to a deep, painful place that didn't even have words. He spent time that day finding language that depicted a deep truth.

The deeper story was this: "This is where Carolyn finds out that I'm not good enough for her."

That's shame. When I let him know that I had expected him to do the more challenging marketing tasks, a deep part of him that he was almost not aware of spoke: "You,

Jim, are not enough for Carolyn". He had pulled away out of that deep sense of shame.

What I had seen as dismissiveness was withdrawal. When a person doesn't feel good enough, they want to disappear.

What I had seen as rudeness and disrespect was a painful effort to hide. Walking away is Jim's way of not being seen.

Shame does not want to be seen.

It had never occurred to me that when Jim left the room, it had its roots in shame. It had never crossed my mind he wasn't good enough for me.

Shame does its powerful thing without regard to the truth.

What happened next is something I couldn't have predicted.

When he told me that walking away was a shame response, I could reach a deeper part of myself that I hadn't known about that also impacted this situation. I could now see the magnitude of my own big reaction when he walked out of the room. Relationships are a dialogue and only at that moment did I realize I hadn't contributed to a positive dynamic myself.

When he walked out of the room, I wasn't calm and connected to walk over to him a few minutes later and, in a friendly way, just check in on his reaction. I had gotten upset instead of just chatting with him about it. I had also been hooked by my own shame.

I had restrained myself (because of my upcoming sermon on marriage) but what I had really wanted to do was blast him. I wanted to blame him. I like words and I held myself back from using all the words to lecture, get defensive, and generally unload.

Shame does that too. When we aren't feeling *good enough*, we look to make the other person smaller. A shame reaction can be the opposite of hiding—it goes on the offense to prove that the feeling of unworthiness is a lie. My choice to not do damage was a form of reducing harm, but it certainly didn't foster connection.

I love my husband for all sorts of reasons, but when he came towards me without the judgement or criticism that shame can bring, I loved him all over again. He had worked through his shame to understand it and now could come to me. He gave us a chance to really repair the damage of the evening before that made our entire relationship more solid.

When Jim opened the door to his own shame, he helped me unlock the door to understand mine.

Being real and authentic in a vulnerable way invites others to do the same.

I heard myself saying: "When you didn't do the marketing calls we had discussed, to me it meant that you were telling me that our discussions don't matter to you. And if our discussions don't matter, then I don't matter." In my world, as a woman, I have experienced men who nod and smile at my ideas but don't take me seriously. Too often that's part of being a woman in our world.

Both Jim and I could be present for each other in that moment. Upon naming the shame, it wasn't hard at all to show up for each other.

And then we had this time to reaffirm our love for each other, and remind each other of *the real*—which is that I love him deeply as he is, and he loves me, as I am.

Jim loves this story—and loves that I tell it in my workshops. When I get home from a keynote speech, he will sometimes ask, almost hopefully: "Did you tell the 'Puffed Wheat Story?'"

Not long ago, I received feedback after a workshop that it was cruel for me to disclose this story that depicts my husband in such a vulnerable light. Other times, when I do a radio interview and tell a story of a struggle I face, my mom will say, "Carolyn, I admire how you are willing to be so vulnerable." She can't quite believe that I will let people into my life with the stories I tell.

Here's the thing. What has now become the "Puffed Wheat Story" in our family is not unique to us. Perhaps the specific details are unique—but the themes are universal. I hear versions of this story every week in my office. This is a story of something that humans all do all the time.

I'm not sure it's particularly vulnerable when it is so particularly, and profoundly, human.

I've always loved stories. I was a voracious reader as a child. My mom used to take us to the library every 3 weeks—that was the period of how long a book could be loaned out. We were allowed to take 6 books out at a time. I always took out the maximum number, and I was generally done all of them well before the allotted time. Sometimes, I was already done a chapter or two by the time we arrived home. I loved good stories. I often read biographies, but loved a good *Nancy Drew* mystery, or *Cherry Ames, Nurse Detective* stories.

My mom and I had a fundamental disagreement. I maintained that a person could both read a book and set the table simultaneously. She insisted that setting the table was a task best done with singular focus. I just knew she couldn't understand my pain at the thought of having to put down a good book when I just *had* to find out what was going to happen next. I could hold the book with one hand and set plates with the other. And, after all, I didn't read at the table *during* the meal. (Though I have vague recollections of having a book on my lap that I could sneak a few peeks at when I thought no one would notice).

I have come to discover that the power of story isn't restricted to books.

You and I create a plethora of stories all the time, unbeknownst to ourselves. Once we recognize the stories we are telling ourselves, we can begin to re-write them.

The recognition of those stories will fundamentally change your connection with other people.

You'll fall in love with seeing and knowing that stories shape your life. You'll invite yourself to tell different stories that are compassionate and understanding towards yourself and others.

We, as humans, neurobiologically, are wired for story. Our brains notice the data and connect the data into stories to keep us alive. Stories are a good thing because, very basically and simply, they help us to not be dead. Our brains use story to notice danger and avoid it.

Once we know how the story can end, it teaches us what is safe and what isn't.

We make sense of our world by knowing the beginning of a story and predicting the next stage. If you are hiking in the desert and you hear a rattle, you freeze and look around for a rattle snake. They are poisonous and the stories you've heard help you write a different ending.

Knowing the end and the beginning can help you predict the middle. If you have a mischievous toddler and they are in another room and you realize, suddenly, it has been suspiciously quiet, you run into the room. Your suspicions are confirmed: it doesn't take a rocket scientist to know what happened when there are random swipes of ketchup on the walls and all over your toddler.

In my part of Canada, the ice gets thick on the lake in winter so trucks can drive little houses onto it so people can go ice fishing in the comfort of these ice fishing shacks. In the spring, when they go out fishing, these ice fisher people will be checking the thickness of the ice. Every year, there are stories of trucks going through the ice. Sometimes, the people escape, barely. Sometimes, they have drowned. Connecting the thickness of the ice with the stories of tragedy helps people stay alive as they get off the ice soon enough. Thin ice is death. Lives are saved every year as people use the stories of what is safe and what is dangerous ice to keep themselves safe.

We don't need a play by play of every detail of a story for us to know what can happen or will happen or has happened. We use our natural smarts to fill in the blanks.

And we don't just fill in the blanks around thin ice or rattlesnakes. We can detect when we might be on "thin ice" in a conversation—and adjust our input. You might:

- Read an email from a colleague and look to make sense of its terseness—and you instantly assume: "They must be angry with me!"

- Make sense of the absence of a cousin from the funeral. "She never liked us anyway."

- Look to understand why there was no thank you for the wedding gift you gave—"Do they think I'm cheap?"

This is the constellation Orion. You can see the three stars that make up its belt.

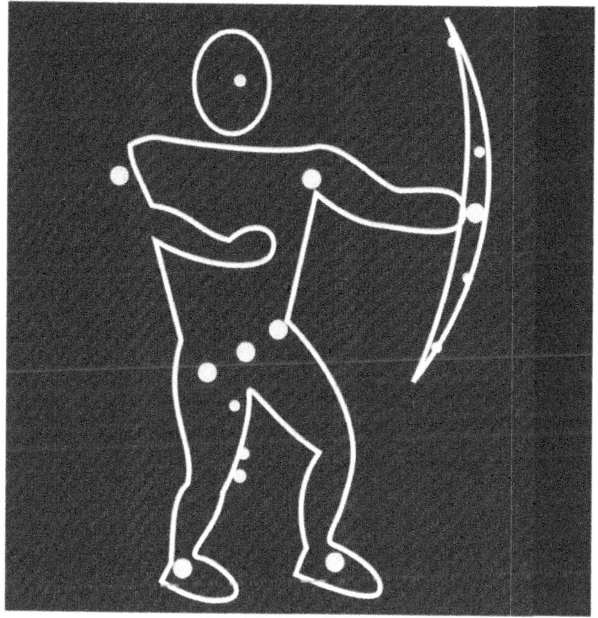

Somehow, people in times past decided it looked like Orion from ancient Greek mythology. It seems to me that it could have been named after a table, or a unicorn or a banana—or any number of characters of ancient cultural stories.

This is what is known in story language as a *conspiracy*.[20] Someone connected the dots in a way that told a story of the archer, Orion.

Our brains are connecting the dots constantly on our behalf beyond our awareness in ways that keep us safe and wise. However, our brains are so eager to connect the dots that they will be sure to connect them first, with accuracy sometimes being secondary. Given the lack of data in between the data points, it may well be quite inaccurate.

Conspiracy theories get a lot of bad press these days. We don't want to be associated with them.

But we all develop conspiracies. I developed a conspiracy when I knew Jim had left the room as an act of dismissive rudeness. He developed a conspiracy about me when he decided my *inevitable, anticipated* disappointment over his lack of phone calls that day meant that he wasn't good enough for me.

Developing conspiracies is a part of the human condition as we look to make sense of our world and keep ourselves safe. Not only in nature, but in our relationships with people.

If we are wired for connection, and connection is as important to us as food, water, and oxygen, we all look to be aware of potential danger that is a sign of disconnection.

In a conversation, I can notice:

- Unusual silences
- Abrupt responses
- Side eye or eye rolling or snickering or chuckling that might be snickering
- Sarcasm
- Criticism
- A deep sigh
- Folded arms
- A camera turned off during a video call

—and then make meaning of it. I have the data: what I said, and what their body just did, and I fill in the blanks with a meaning that makes sense to me.

The meaning I often make is designed to help me stay safe. My brain would rather be wrong with a story than have no story at all. And if connection is as important as food, water, and oxygen (you know the drill by now), then the possibility of disconnection is where my brain will go first. I will make up a shame-based story as my brain wants to keep me safe. It directs my action in the next moment of interaction, and it will my shape future interactions with this person—and maybe other people too.

In my brain's rush to keep me safe, it makes up stories like:

- He never liked me anyway
- She always had a thing out for me
- He never takes me seriously
- They think they are prettier/richer/smarter than me
- Who am I to think that they would be respectful towards me?

As I rush to a shame-based story, excluding all other, many possibilities that have nothing to do with judgement, criticism, or shame:

- The email is short because she is overwhelmed with personal and professional responsibilities
- His eyes did something funny because he had something in one of them

- He was breathing deeply because he had just totalled his car that morning and he was flooded
- She folds her arms because she is protecting herself in the discussion—having had painful relationships that are being made fresh again in the conversation
- He is sarcastic because he is feeling his own shame in response to what you just said.

I used to work in hospitals and residential care centers with people who had cognitive issues and required support because of their poor memory. Occasionally, I would encounter a person with Korsakoff's syndrome. Korsakoff's syndrome is most often brought on by chronic alcoholism and is tragic.

Relating to folks with Korsakoff's syndrome was quite fun, in the moment. I really enjoyed the experience. While I knew that the patient was living in hospital, having hospital food, and confined to the unit, they would tell vivid stories of what they had done that day. I would hear stories of golfing, time with friends, lavish meals out that they remembered. The conversations were generally pleasant and fun as I could enjoy the patient enjoy the memory.

Those events didn't happen, but the patients who had Korsakoff's actually remembered that these experiences. This is known as *confabulation*: a lie told honestly.[21]

I have been told by a friend that when people don't know me well, they have thought me a pretentious snob.

Ouch.

The reason given is that I don't walk across the room to shake a stranger's hand and introduce myself and get to know them. In a crowded room where I don't know people, I don't *work the crowd* to get to know lots of people.

The story they tell themselves is that I'm standoffish and act like I'm too good for them. They feel that I am telling others that they are beneath me. My friend hears that story and immediately knows it is a confabulation. It is a lie told honestly.

I believe that others really believe this.

It can be difficult for people to wrap their head around the fact that I am an introvert and crowded rooms with strangers aren't really my thing. I may speak on the radio and to large crowds, but my jam is having meaningful conversation with just one or two people off to the side.

It *is* true that I am not moving about the room greeting many people—but the real reason is very different from the one that some people might decide is the truth.

Again, when we confabulate, we tend to do so in a way that is either accepting our own unworthiness-shame, or fighting against the feeling that we are being devalued—shame.

Brené Brown says, "'I'm not enough' is one of my go-to narratives when I'm hurt. It's the equivalent of my comfy jeans."[22] Our brains automatically use conspiracy and confabulation to weave a story about shame. We may not like it, or want it, but it's very human to do so.

From my years in the counselling room, I've come to see that this has two major implications:

1. I need to check the stories I'm telling myself and notice that my default is one connected to shame. I can invite myself to see that there may be anoth-

er way of looking at things. I can support myself and remind myself that I'm biased towards a shame story. It challenges me to invite myself to check out those stories: "The story I tell myself is that..." I am better able to avoid stonewalling, defensiveness, criticism, and all sorts of other conversation killers—or at least apologize for them in a timelier manner.

2. I can safely assume that an out-of-proportion or surprising or hurtful reaction by another in a relationship with me likely has something to do with the story they are telling themselves. Further, in the moment, they won't be aware of that story—because we tell ourselves stories so automatically, we aren't taking time to think it through. Remember, the purpose of storytelling is to not die—that storytelling happens so quickly because it's as if one's life is on the line.

This second point has been a game changer as I've worked with couples in marriage therapy.

- He reacts angrily to her frustration around their credit card debt. With conversation, we discover he feels ashamed that he isn't providing enough for his family, which leads to debt. She doesn't blame him for his income as cause for her reaction to the debt, which initially makes his reaction hard to understand. Once this shame story is exposed, they are better able to connect and confront their debt issues collaboratively.

- A manager has a conversation with an employee who is repeatedly late for work. The employee gen-

> erally does excellent work. The employee erupts when the manager has the meeting about the tardiness and stomps out of the room. The employee feels, at that moment, that the only measure of effectiveness is their punctuality in a manner that feels grossly unfair.

When clients can move from being annoyed and frustrated, or scared, or disenchanted with a relationship and move to compassion by opening the possibility of shame creating the story, they can be calm and grounded as they re-enter the conversation.

This requires a generosity which is courageous.

"The story I tell myself..." is a powerful tool to process disruption in relationship. As we are aware of the undercurrents of hidden shame in a relationship, we gain the ability to make choices about that shame. The shame is no longer pulling strings behind the scenes—you make the choices and decrease its power to run the relationship.

"Owning our story and loving ourselves through that process is the bravest thing we'll ever do." **Brené Brown**

I used to think that good relationships were about laughter and "kumbaya" feelings.
Now I know that quality relationships are borne out of candid and brave conversations.

WIRED FOR CONNECTION

Less kumbaya, more discomfort

I used to think that good relationships were about laughter and "kumbaya" feelings. Now I know that quality relationships are borne out of candid and brave conversations.

HEATED DISCUSSIONS MAKE MOST of us feel uncomfortable, me included. Early on in my career as a therapist, I remember sitting with a couple who were pointing their fingers at each other with raised voices. They were trying to talk over each other repeatedly. I remember thinking to myself, "These people *really* need to see a therapist." In other words, my body wanted someone else to look after this discussion.

It was a split second later when I realized I was it! I was their therapist, and it was up to me to find a way to stop the destruction!

As uncomfortable as I was, and as out of my depth as I felt in the moment, I needed to intervene and be a presence to them that would increase productivity in the discussion. (Yes, therapists are people too, and experiencing relational tension and the deliberate choice to lean in, is a *manual override* of our own natural tendencies, especially early on in our careers.)

I didn't seek to make them comfortable or stop the pain. Those uncomfortable conversations are important. I took a deep breath and plunged on into the discomfort with them. I wasn't going to let them avoid the discomfort. Neither would I let them go into it without me. I have the metaphorical flashlight that will make walking into the unknown possible.

When I have more than one person in my counselling office and they start a difficult conversation, my pulse and blood pressure feel the pull to rise. I still often have to take a deep breath and remind myself: "Sixty beats a minute. I can stay calm and present as their tension goes up. This engagement with each other can be a good thing if I can be present with them and help shape this dialogue to help them learn about each other. They have a real opportunity to connect if they can find a way to reach each other even when they have differences—and they will always have differences."

I still have moments when the conflict in the room raises my own internal temperature. But I've walked with enough clients through enough tense moments to know that the rainbow only comes out after the storm. The clients who never even let their relationship get cloudy cheat themselves out of the beauty.

Discomfort doesn't kill us—even though sometimes it feels like it just might.

Relational discomfort doesn't end our lives.

But avoiding it can end the relationship.

Imagine yourself in dance class. The dance teacher very carefully demonstrates the footwork with her partner, describing where your feet and your partner's feet will go. The teacher starts off by demonstrating 6 beats of dance steps: 1, 2, 3, 4, 5, 6 and starts again at 1, looping through the count repeatedly in the same routinized rhythm. It's beautiful when the teacher and the partner do the pattern—with remarkable fluidity in their partnership.

Then you try it with your partner. You stumble through the first several attempts, but eventually get the pattern to navigate through the 6 steps. You keep doing it, and it works.

Or, at least, it looks like it does from across the room. What you are acutely aware of is that on beat 4 of every pattern, your partner steps on your foot. While your foot goes forward, so does your partner's foot—and crushes yours.

It hurt a little the first time. More the second time. After several rounds of being stepped on, the pain is now building. There will be a bruise.

But you say nothing.

You wouldn't do that, would you? Allow your partner to step on your foot repeatedly over and over? That wouldn't happen, couldn't happen—could it?

And yet in the dance of relationships, I see it happening regularly with people who come in to talk through a relationship that isn't working. Their feelings or approach are getting stepped on regularly, but they continue to tolerate the painful part of the relationship.

- A manager is regularly harsh when giving feedback. She is naturally a gruff sort of person, but it has a cutting effect on you.

- A friend often cancels plans on short notice after you have carefully carved a space to get together.

- A neighbour, intending to be kind, prunes your bushes when he prunes his—except you like to do the job—and you prefer your bushes fuller than how he prunes them.

- Your spouse spends too many weekends volunteering with the local community centre, and you are home alone with the kids.

- Your girlfriend calls you by a nickname she finds adorable—and you find grating.

Sometimes, these matters are trifling. They are truly not a significant issue for you, and it's easy to let the matter slide. It doesn't interfere with your relationship.

However, often a person only pretends it is not a big deal. It matters. And here is where it gets interesting in therapy. Despite the pain of being repeatedly hurt in a patterned sort of way, nothing is mentioned.

And when I ask why they allow themselves to be hurt, the answer is generally one of two responses:

The first response: They will, in some way, be adamant in saying: "*I don't want to hurt their feelings*". People find it so necessary to avoid the discomfort of another person's discomfort, they continue to tolerate the pain that is recreated repeatedly in the relationship.

They tolerate ongoing pain for themselves by choosing to not address the "foot stomping moment in the dance pattern" of the relationship.

What I find painful is this: most of us would like to know when we are, in some ways, stepping on another person's toes. I want to know when I cause pain to someone so we can figure out a way to not make it happen. Don't you?

Over time, the toll of the painful patterns adds up. What I have often heard is that the pain in that particular step of the relationship becomes more significant than the benefits of the relationship. It is at this point that consideration is given to ending the relationship or some sort of drastic action:

- I guess I'll have to look for another job
- I can't keep making plans if my friend keeps cancelling. I'll stop getting together with her.
- I guess I'll just get rid of the shrubs and plant grass because I don't like how bare they are with the harsh pruning.
- If I'm on my own all the time, I may as well not be married.

The problem is unaddressed. Your pain increases, perhaps along with resentment and frustration. You change in the relationship because you are doing what you can to avoid the pain without really addressing it—often pulling away, withdrawing, avoiding.

When the other person senses you are avoiding the step in the relationship that causes the pain, they don't know it's the pain you are avoiding. It will feel like you are avoiding **them**.

I've had clients tell me that they will have to end their marriage because of a painful pattern in the relationship which they have not actively addressed in a relationship. They want to avoid hurting the other person, so the problems remain unaddressed until the relationship is intolerable. (Spoiler alert: the spouse does not avoid pain in this instance—the ending of a marriage is crushing.)

The paradox, I suspect, is quite apparent: to avoid hurting your friend or mother or sister or friend or wife, you don't mention what isn't working for you. But they do get hurt with you avoiding or leaving the relationship at some level—they just won't understand why.

The second response: If a person can be somehow willing to risk saying something brave that might be experienced as hurtful, *they themselves risk being hurt* by the other person's reaction. Their message is something like: "I'm scared to bring it up because the other person will dismiss my concern, mock it, or even end the relationship with me. I don't know what will happen, but what if they get mad at me?"

When naming a painful dynamic in a relationship, it becomes very uncertain. How will the other person react?

- My mother comments on my weight each time we visit. What if she is furious with me if I ask her to stop? What if she doubles down and says it even more often?

- My boss makes fun of my ethnicity. Will I be fired if

I say something?

- My friend makes a fool of himself when we go watch a game because of how plastered he gets, and I have to drive him home. Who will I go to a game with if he finds someone else to go with because he doesn't like that I say something?

- Our credit card balance keeps climbing. Will my partner give me the silent treatment, or worse yet, say it's over if I bring it up?

The feeling of fear is real. No one likes to be hurt. Bringing up a pain point is hard for everyone. There is no guarantee how a person will respond to your concern.

However, that fear is often connected to devaluing oneself. When one doesn't recognize one's own inherent worth in the relationship or as a human being, one can either *overestimate the magnitude of the negative reaction* **or** *consign oneself to a relationship that is beneath one's dignity.*

In the former, you are not allowing for the fact that you are important in the relationship, and while there will be discomfort in bringing something difficult up, the other person is open to making your life better—because they care about you. They don't want to hurt you. They don't want to lose you—in little or big ways.

In the latter, the reaction of the other may be that mean or destructive. They may not be willing to change—or worse, smash their foot a little harder on each foot stomping step of the dance of the relationship. There is an unspoken expectation to put up with pain as part of being in the relationship.

A client says to me: "If I tell my friend that her racist jokes bother me, she will probably tell me that she's not going to change. She will say she is just kidding and I'm too sensitive. She might stop being friends with me." What often ensues, in a therapy session, is a painful but important conversation: "If your friend isn't willing to hear how she is hurting you and be responsive to it, perhaps we should explore the quality of the friendship?"

When you tolerate inappropriate or painful behavior of another as the price of admission for the relationship, is it a relationship you really want to have? Are you really in meaningful relationship if you edit yourself to talk about the hard stuff because you do not trust your friend will hear you? Sometimes, the response is a great one:

- Clients will tell me that if they raise a concern with their manager, they fear that they will be punished with fewer opportunities or even dismissed from employment. However, when the client chooses to raise it with the employer, to their surprise, they find that the employer is eager to make the change because the employee is valuable to the company.

- A client is terrified to ask about finances with her partner. We broach the conversation in a session. The partner says, "I look after it all to let you focus on other things. If you want to know about the money, let's go home and I'll show you!

- My husband, Jim, called me "cutie" when we started dating. I'm sorry, but I'm just not a "cutie". Just no. Our relationship felt tender, as all relationships do in the beginning, but I let him know that this endearment did not work for me. To my surprise, he simply said, "Thank you for telling me." And never said it again. To me, that was one more "green flag" that our relationship could develop further. He was responsive to me, and I loved that.

I could tell you a thousand beautiful and brutal stories about uncomfortable conversations that have changed the course of a relationship in my therapy room. Those non-kumbaya conversations feel high risk, but have the potential to create understanding, empathy, and compassion. The walls of the therapy room hold the tears and fears of these conversations as people leaned into the discomfort. The walls also hold the relief and intimacy of clients as they emerged out the other side closer because they weathered the storm and enjoy the intimacy that is now available.

Tip from Jim: If there is an occasion where a family or friend gives you feedback about how, metaphorically, you are stepping on their foot on every 4 count in your relationship dance, the optimum response is, "Thank you for telling me." No need to rationalize, explain, defend or protest. Expressing gratitude for the courageous feedback will affirm the risk the other person invested in to improve the relationship.

I consider these uncomfortable discussions in therapy *fun*. When my kids were in high school and we would talk about our days at the supper table, and I would say it had been a *fun* day, they would roll their eyes, knowing what I meant. My children were (and are) convinced I have a very warped view of *fun*. What they don't see, however, is the lightness of spirit clients have when they have a difficult conversation that is awkward and uncomfortable. It's a sacred event, really, when folks dare to initiate a hard conversation.

While it can look like cruelty to mention something painful to another, it is really a sign of deep relationship investment. Having hard conversations is well—hard!

Uncomfortable conversations are the sort of thing that only happens **when the relationship matters more than the discomfort.**

What would happen if you would consider it as a significant investment in the relationship when a friend asks you, "Can I talk to you about something that's bothering me?"

Susan says: "It bothers me that you don't want to spend time with my family. They are important to me, and you are pulling away from them."

Bob responds: "You're making a big deal out of something that isn't a big deal."

Susan: "Actually, it is a big deal—to me. I love my family and I want to enjoy being with them. I don't like feeling like I'm dragging you there or not going at all."

Bob: "I like your family, too. Really."

Susan: "That's hard for me to believe. You have been making excuses lately when my parents invite us over."

Bob: "I really do like them. It's just uncomfortable for me to be around them."

Susan: "But they are great people. You used to really like them. I used to think you would invite yourself to come over to watch the game because you liked watching it with my dad more than me. *The story I tell myself is* that you don't like them anymore, and now I will find myself having to choose between you and them."

(Actually, she didn't use the sentence starter, "The story I tell myself is..." but I wanted to show you how well it works. So, let's just pretend she did. It is essentially what she meant.)

Here's the situation: Susan and Bob have come for counselling as newlyweds. They have a choice of only celebrating their strengths or working on a speed bump in their relationship. Not only does working through this concern help them figure this situation out, it also gives them practice working through an issue rather than avoiding it and hoping it will go away.

I'm giving a shortened version of it here, because in session, this took several minutes. I gave Susan some support to continue to raise her concerns even when he tried to change the topic, blow it off or minimize her concern. I helped Bob understand that even though it was hard to talk about, I understood that there was a more important reason to avoid them than to spend time with them, even if it wasn't easily apparent.

I also helped him with a bit of language—because, as mentioned in an earlier chapter, shame hates words being wrapped around it. With a bit of stumbling over his words, and a couple of attempts, and some coaching, he could articulate: "Yes, I really like your parents. A lot. But they aren't just nice people to hang out with now. You are their youngest daughter, and your dad isn't just a pal anymore. He's the dad of the woman I married. I think he might be judging me. Maybe I don't make enough money. Maybe he doesn't think I'm very smart. Maybe he thinks I'm not good enough for you. I get so in my head about all this, I can't think of anything to say. I'm nervous and anxious. And then, for sure, I'm certain he thinks I suck as a son-in-law. Worse yet, I figured if I would drink alcohol, I'd be less anxious.

And it worked—but then I started acting stupid and saying dumb things. So, if I just avoid him, I don't have to feel this feeling that I have inside myself when I'm around him. This feeling like I don't measure up to the man he wants for his daughter to spend her life with is a feeling I avoid."

That's when it got beautiful for them. It was *fun* for me. Susan had a chance to talk to Bob about what her dad has said about Bob to her—and it was positive. She found out about her husband's fears as he had just joined their family in ways that endeared him to her even more. To know her father's opinion of Bob mattered so much to Bob further had him understand his love for her, and how seriously he took wanting to be a great husband. She thanked him for telling her, knowing it wasn't easy.

It was a relief for him. After being candid about something so vulnerable, he had feared judgement and ridicule.

He got love instead.

It's not easy to look at the fork in the road: Kumbaya to the right, messy dialogue on the left. It's a risk and going to kumbaya is easier. Every time.

Easier—but inauthentic.

Easier—but not as rich.

Easier—but sets the relationship up for deterioration in the long haul.

Going left—to messy dialogue—gives your relationship an opportunity for healing, growth, and depth. Given that we are wired for connection—taking the risk to address the concern, be vulnerable, work out the knots in the relationship is worth it.

Relational discomfort grows connection when it is done respectfully, gently and with consideration for who the other person is and how they hear things. The number one safe assumption to make is this: When you have a conversation about something tough, the other person's reflex will probably to be pulled into a shame reaction.

In other words, using our metaphor from earlier, when you say, "On every beat 4 of the dance of my relationship, you step on my foot," their knee jerk reaction will be to say, "I didn't mean to" or "Are you sure?" or "You might be mistaken. I'm not the sort of person who would step on your toes." Or even, "How dare you accuse me of stepping on your toes. Do you think I'd actually do that?"

The reaction is without compassion—it is about looking after themselves—not your foot. This is the normal reaction to expect.

It does not mean it was a mistake to raise the topic.

Might I suggest setting up a non-Kumbaya conversation while simultaneously presuming the reflex reaction will occur? You can prepare the soil of the interaction to create a more genuine conversation.

You might try one of these:

- Do you have a few minutes for me to bring something up that has been bothering me lately? It might be hard to hear, so I'm just asking you to listen and ask a question or two.

- I know you are for my good. I can feel it. And it is out of knowing that you care about me, that I wanted to talk about something that's hard. This is an opportunity to make our friendship even better than it is.

- I believe in that our relationship can handle hard conversations. I like to think we are the sort of people that can raise an issue with each other, trusting that we can do better work as colleagues when we know what works and doesn't work.

- If I told you something hard right now, do you have the capacity to hear it just as my experience, and know that I am not saying anything bad about who you are?

After you start the conversation with a gentle start up—something like above or whatever works for you—then focus on behavior rather than character.

Avoid extremes like, "always" and "never".

Imagine yourself on the same side of the table as the other person in the conversation—with the issue being something the two of you will tackle together.

When the other person finds it a hard conversation, agree with them that it is hard—because it is. And then take a deep breath and continue in a way that allows the two of you to continue to muddle your way through.

It might be that the other person finds it difficult to have these conversations and immediately moves into shame. They might need some time. You might need to continue the conversation hours later or even the next day, clarifying what you are and are not saying.

You might even have to "back the conversation" up. If it is too hard to talk about how your foot is hurt on each "4 count" in the dance of your relationship, you might need to talk about how you are going to talk about hard things. This conversation is best done when both of you are in a good space. This can be done with a partner, a friend, a colleague, or a sibling.

You can ask: "Our relationship is between two humans—we both make mistakes. I'd like us to have the best relationship possible. From time to time, there are going to be matters that arise that deserve a conversation. If I ever wanted to talk about something about us, what would work for you for me to be able to do it? I think it is a part of every relationship to have a way to work things out so it can improve."

It won't always be neat and tidy. Sometimes, it will be messy for a while.

It's ok to not be ok as you are working to be ok.

If you are intent on improving the relationship, the hard of it all won't be easy, but it won't last forever.

Messy conversations are like tangling root systems together. It's not tidy, but it leads to greater connectivity.

"Relationships don't last because of the good times; they last because the hard times were handled with love and care." **Anmol Andore**

I used to think that thinking
about and caring for oneself
was selfish and self-centred.
Now I know that
self-compassion sets me up to
be more caring in relationships.

WIRED FOR CONNECTION

Self compassion isn't self-indulgent

I used to think that thinking about and caring for oneself was selfish and self-centred. Now I know that self-compassion sets me up to be more caring in relationships.

I STARTED INTENTIONALLY learning about self-compassion almost a decade ago. The research in the field of self-compassion was exploding and part of being a competent therapist was to understand the research. The science was compelling and if the evidence said that it was effective for my clients, I would learn it and help them apply it.

I fought against the idea of self-compassion for myself for years. I was raised in an environment of putting others endlessly first. During my childhood, my mother would fall asleep as soon as she sat down in the evenings, as she was often running on empty. My parents raised my brothers and I with a family ethic of service to others, both formally and informally. If there was a need and we could meet it, we should try. Our parents taught us that play happened after the work was done—and the work was never done.

I registered for a course on self-compassion offered at a local hospital featuring Dr. Kristin Neff, who literally wrote the book on Self-Compassion.[23] The most powerful lesson I learned about self-compassion wasn't learned at the course about self-compassion, but in the course of life.

After I registered for the two-day workshop, I spent time on describing self-compassion. I viewed her TEDx talk[24] a few times to become familiar with some of her most basic principles to really prepare me to get the most out of the course she would be teaching. I can see now—I was working hard (in my head) to understand self-compassion (which is an action of the heart).

My clients understand me on this: so often, we get something in our head and our heart can't translate into action. Our bodies don't enact the truth of what the head knows.

Being a therapist, I get to see that I am not alone.

To practice self-compassion, at its core, is to use three skills: self-kindness, mindfulness, and acknowledging common humanity.[25] They are easy to learn (in your head), but difficult to practice (in your heart).

First, self-compassion is talking to yourself like you would talk to a friend. Ask yourself this question: "If I were to talk to others the way I talk to myself, how would they respond?"

For myself, the answer is: "I wouldn't have any friends—no one should allow themselves to be spoken to by another person that way!"

Jim, my husband, has more than once, when I'm muttering to myself about how stupid I am for letting the cookies get too brown in the oven, or forgetting to mark something on the calendar, asked me: "Please don't talk to yourself that way when you make a mistake. I make mistakes too, and if that's what you say after a mistake, I'm worried you will talk to me like that."

Truth is, I would never talk to him the way I talk to myself. I wouldn't think of talking that way to anybody. Ever.

And yet, I say these things to myself.

My guess is that you do, too.

Imagine a child who performed poorly on a math test—and you towered over them to yell at him for his poor performance. You shook your finger in his face in a menacing way. You shamed him for being a bad person—not just having a poor grade. You told that child that he was an idiot and this lousy grade proved that he was fundamentally lazy and a burden to everyone he knows. You chided him to do better with an implicit threat that he would get even more ire should his next performance not be much better.

And then, right after this chewing out—you gave them another math test.

What are the chances he would do better?

Nil.

None of us do well with verbal violence—our adrenaline goes up and we are in a state of panic. It's hard to do anything with clarity and proficiency when in such a state of alarm.

It makes little sense to scold and yell and shame and menace and name-call and then expect better performance, doesn't it? And yet, that is often the sequence of events internally as we work through a difficult spot.

This is hard on the most basic of friendships: the one you have with yourself. Part of being the best friend/manager/parent/spouse you can be to others is to have a friendly and supportive relationship with yourself.

This isn't just psychological mumbo-jumbo. When you can't practice self-kindness:

- You have set yourself up for: I dare not make a mistake. I need to deny all errors because I cannot tolerate the internal battering I provide myself. That means that others can't point out ways in which you can be better. Others keep their mouth shut instead of giving you feedback that could improve your connection with each other.

- During a tough conversation, the yelling in your own head can get so loud you cannot hear the other person. That internal noise behaves as annoying static that interferes with dialogue between people.

- As you enter a meeting, your own self-criticism may have you edit yourself so ideas that might be useful to the group will never be heard.

The world loses out on positive interactions with you when you can't practice self-kindness.

A day or two before the workshop, I received an email giving typical workshop information about parking, a map to find the room in the large center it was being held, and information about what to expect. The email instructed attendees to wear comfortable clothes and to bring a *yoga mat.*

Ugh.

I love learning, but I like to learn with my head when I'm around other people: teach my brain what it needs to know when I'm around strangers. I had every intention of bringing my laptop computer and typing all sorts of knowledge gems into a word document as I soaked up the knowledge she would impart. I like to do my "heart learning" on my own, or with a few safe and trusted folk. I am a contemplative type and have deliberate contemplative practices I find deeply meaningful and significant, but I'm not a regular yoga/meditation type. I had not realized that this workshop would involve carrying out contemplative, experiential activities—with strangers all around.

The idea of the mat suggested we would do exercise/meditations that would explore our inner world, have us practice self-compassion at the workshop. Didn't take a rocket scientist—or an experienced therapist—to know I would have unknown degrees of vulnerability during these two days as they would expect me to *yoga my way* into learning about self-compassion. (Yes, yoga is a verb here, and I don't apologize.)

As I thought about it, I realized it would only make sense that a workshop on self-compassion would include elements of experiencing, practicing, and exploring self-compassion.

That didn't mean I was going to like it!

Considering this yoga equipment request and all that it implied, I was now quite nervous about what would happen. The therapists at the office that week chuckled at my anxiety as I wandered about the office in my agitated state.

I gnashed my teeth and complained about the need for a mat, when I knew all I really wanted to do was take notes.

On my way home from work the day before the course, I decided I would be proactive and head into my vulnerability head on. Though the information email said there would be a limited number of mats available, they encouraged folks to bring their own. I told myself I would purchase a mat.

The story I told myself was I wanted to be generous. I would ostensibly ensure the mats they had available for others as an act of generosity. But I wasn't fooling anybody—least of all myself. In actuality, I was armoring up against my vulnerability. I was going to saunter into that workshop like a pro, with a mat rolled up under my arm like it belonged there.

And that would demonstrate to all strangers who might judge that I looked like belonged there. Because by now, I was feeling very much like I would not belong.

Just before heading to the store, I looked once more at the instructions. I realized an error: what I remembered as saying "yoga mat" said, "meditation mat and cushion". I googled that, to make sure that yoga mats and meditation mats are the same thing.

They. So. Aren't.

The warm rush of heat crawled up my neck and filled my cheeks as I sat there, humiliated. I had very nearly prepared myself incorrectly. I had very nearly purchased a yoga mat when what was called for was a meditation mat. Imagine something circular and a foot-fluffy thick—this was asked for. My intended purchase was a spongey thin rectangle that rolled up.

I was in trouble. Or so I thought.

The second part of self-compassion is mindfulness. Mindfulness, as used here, is about paying attention:

- To your body—what is it feeling? Are your cheeks feeling hot? Is your head feeling like it is in a vice? Is your chest tight? Does your stomach feel leaden? Is your skin crawling?

- To your emotions. If you are angry, what is underneath that anger? Are you hungry—or hangry? Are you over tired? Are you jealous, scared, lonely?

- To the situation. Who is saying what? What are alternate interpretations of what they are saying? What are they dynamics at play? Are there safety concerns? What is happening to the history?

- To the history. Has this happened before? What happens in these sorts of situations for you? Are you falling into old patterns? Are they? Are you assuming old patterns without creating space for a new way forward?

Self-compassion helps you be aware of what is happening in ways that allow you to be good to yourself and good to others:

- At the end of the day, now, I am exhausted. I'm not sure I can be my best self to respond to that email from my mother complaining about my child's behavior last weekend. Tomorrow, when I'm fresher, I'll do it.

- This manager is using words and tone like my father used to use when he was upset with me. Perhaps I'm reacting to my dad even more than my manager in this moment. Let me take a deep breath and work to stay present.

- I'm feeling vulnerable because of my job performance review meeting today. I'm going to let my partner and the kids know that I'm likely to be sensitive to criticism today and I'm going to watch to make sure I don't blast anyone giving me more negative feedback today. It's possible I'll lose if my toddler tells me he doesn't like how I stack his blocks.

The other part of mindfulness is perspective. We are complex creatures: I can both be upset and watch myself with interest be upset.

When I do live television interviews, I still get nervous. I worry I will blank out and have nothing to say. I worry the interviewer will throw a curve-ball question and I won't know how to respond. I worry I will fall on my face and ruin my career.

And I practice mindfulness as I say to myself: "Hey, Carolyn, you are doing that thing where you are catastrophizing. You did this last time and the time before you did a TV interview, remember? They went ok, maybe even went well. You're doing the nervous thing that you generally do. Go ahead and feel it but remember that you always have gotten through them ok—and this one will be fine too—even if you're not feeling it."

Mindful self-compassion talk doesn't make an uncomfortable feeling go away, but it does somehow make it more tolerable.

Self-compassion reminds me I am more than my thoughts and feelings. I may have a jealous part of me, but I am not jealousy incarnate. When a person feels angry, they may be angry because of injustice—which comes from a place of caring and love. A person can *feel* resentment rather than *being* resent-full.

I had a chorus of lines rushing through my head:

- Do you realize how close you came to making a fool—no, make that—a *complete* fool of yourself?

- What were you trying to pull, making it look like you belonged at this workshop?

- What kind of mental health professional can't tell the difference between a yoga mat and a mediation mat? They will all see that you shouldn't even be a therapist!

- It would be so much easier not to go. Wait a minute, is that a cough coming on? (Please, can I start feeling sick before tomorrow morning?)

These tumultuous painful thoughts came down to this: "Who do you think you are?"

I was not doing well.

The third component of self compassion is understanding common humanity.

I am not perfect. Neither are you. Nor is a single other human soul on the earth, in the past, present, or future. We all make mistakes. Hurting is human. We all struggle.

When I have been inappropriately sharp with my child, my tendency is to go into shame and self-judgement. My negative self-talk goes wild when I fail in the most important role of my life: that of mother. "I'm the world's *worst* mother. I have screwed up his life forever. He doesn't have a chance with a mother like me. What a horrible person I am." No perspective, no grounding in the truth of all mothers everywhere in all moments of history: we all get tired, grumpy and are less than perfect parents.

Understanding the "common humanity" part of self-compassion acknowledges I am not uniquely bad as I deal with inevitable flaws that arise within myself. It is part of the shared human experience to have flaws and screw ups. I can expect that when I have messy relationships, it is because I am human. I will, inevitably, contribute negatively to the dynamics in some way.

My tendency—and likely yours too—is to think: "I am uniquely bad. I'm the only one that makes mistakes like this."

In other words, I need to hide my flawed humanity so that others don't find out.

It is in those moments that self-compassion invites me to recognize my humanity.

This third component of self-compassion plays an important role in at least two ways at this moment. Back to my example of when I mess up as a mom: As I remind myself that all other mothers are imperfect and make mistakes,

I can move from *shame* (I am bad) to *guilt* (I have done something bad). This allows for 2 things:

1. An apology: I can go to my son and own my behavior. I can model to him what an adult does by taking responsibility and repairing the mistake. I can contribute to his own sense of wellbeing because he doesn't have to wonder if what he did deserved that sort of response.

2. I can talk about it with other mothers. When I recognize that others also struggle with their strong emotions towards their children, I don't have to hide my mistake. They too, know what it is like to be too angry with a child. It is not ok to be too harsh—but it is human. I don't think there is a parent alive who has not been pushed past their limits and expressed anger in a way that is too sharp. As I speak with other mothers, they remind me I'm human. They empathize, provide care to me, and share their own stories. I relax—and when I do so, I'm better able to go back to my son to be the mom I want to be for him. As we share challenges, we also share strategies and solutions so I can go in with more resourcing to handle myself when I am upset, or to steer his behavior more effectively in creative ways. The brainstorming between moms as we share is brilliant.

Often my clients tell me about what they are feeling, and then how they feel about what they are feeling. Or how they are thinking something and having then also have thoughts about what they are thinking. They often rush to reassure me they aren't crazy—it's just busy in their heads.

They have feelings about their feelings.

I get that. And now that was happening to me.

While one part of my brain is berating me viciously, there is another part of my brain able to find the humour in how hard I was being as I was preparing myself for a workshop on, duh, *self-compassion*. I could see I was in a shame spiral. Even before the course, I could recognize that my self-judgement was getting away on me and I was perceiving myself as *not enough*. I had already watched the video on the core features of self-compassion, so I worked on:

1. Recognizing that I was hurting and trying to understand what was happening inside me. I was being mindful of the embarrassment, shyness, desire-to-fit-in, etc. that I was experiencing.

2. Trying to be a kind friend to myself, extending compassion and kindness with soft and gentle tone with soothing words of comfort: "You were trying to do something good for yourself in buying that mat, and that's important", "You were smart enough to check before you got the wrong mat. Good on you!", "This is hard, isn't it?", "This is often how you get worked up before a workshop, and it is often ok. You're just doing what you do when you are going somewhere on your own. This reaction is just what happens before something like this."

3. Reminding myself that this was part of the human condition; that we all make mistakes. I repeatedly reminded myself that it was highly likely I was not uniquely ignorant of the differences between yoga mats and meditation mats. I reminded myself that if I ever met someone else who didn't know the difference between the two pieces of equipment,

> I wouldn't judge them as worthless, so perhaps I should re-evaluate how hard I was being on myself.

It. Didn't. Work.

I tried these strategies of self-compassion, and they were utterly ineffective.

Completely out of proportion to what the situation called for, I was still feeling awful about the whole thing. I was catastrophizing the experience to a ridiculous degree, and even being aware of this didn't help in bringing me back to a more appropriate level of distress.

My head knew I was being ridiculous—but that didn't stop my body from continuing to beat myself up. My stomach was in turmoil. My head was hot.

In the middle of my shame and self-berating, a friend called me and I told her this story. We laughed together at my story. She wasn't laughing at me. She laughed with me. Louise understood and didn't berate me. She didn't try talking me out of it either. Louise told me she has gotten carried away too. It didn't have this powerful feeling of panic/distress/shame go away, but it helped with perspective.

At this point, I was berating myself for having the audacity to go to a workshop on self-compassion, believing firmly already in its value, and using the approach with clients and at this moment, being spectacularly unsuccessful in using it effectively for myself.

With this, the intensity of self-criticism ratcheted up exponentially. Even as another part of me could see how I was quite over the top on my reaction, I continued to rebuke myself for multiple layers of errors.

I had given up all attempts to get anything done that evening. This internal battle completely hijacked me, and I gave in to the need to explore and understand this reaction.

At one point, suddenly, somehow in one corner of my brain, I remembered:

I hadn't taken the workshop yet.

Over the course of the next half hour, this concept (which must seem stunningly obvious to you, dear reader) spread from that nook to infiltrate the rest of my brain—and then it spread into my body. The knot loosened.

I was going to the workshop to learn about these principles. I know myself well enough to be aware I always get nervous before going to a two-day event where I don't know if I will know anybody there, and interaction with others will be a part of the experience. I worry about who I will sit with? Will it be ok? Will they like me? Will they think I'm good enough? Etc.

The anxiety over all these intimidating factors was coming out over this ridiculous mat. I could now recognize shame was having a party inside of Carolyn.

Like many, I have perfectionist leanings. Like all, I struggle with shame—that feeling of not being worthy of love and belonging. And like usual, I was expecting myself to be excellent at it right away. Even before I'd gone to the workshop. I was beating myself up for not knowing something before I went to the course to learn it.

I know that doesn't make sense. But I also know that most of us are hard on ourselves for reasons that make little sense once we gently and carefully tease apart what is really happening internally.

And at this realization, I found myself able to soothe myself with understanding and compassion and loving kindness. I didn't have to be good at this yet. I could go as someone who had something to learn. It was OK to have room to grow at this. Now I could see a silver lining: the workshop fee was money well spent because I just showed myself how I really needed to learn this stuff for myself, not only to use with my clients!

I can't say I wasn't still a little nervous and apprehensive about the whole thing that evening. I was, but I showed up the next morning. Walking into a room of strangers wasn't easy, but they weren't the sharks I set them up to be. The other participants were kind and chatty. The teaching was great. I learned a lot. I met some great people and had some fabulous conversations in our groups exploring our experience. It was a fantastic experience.

The postscript to my panic over yoga equipment: To my surprise, I discovered something that tickled my sense of humour, and will be a lifelong lesson in being gentle with myself and not making critical assumptions.

A few people brought "meditation" equipment—the cushy, very fluffy round cushions—but many, many more brought the good old conventional yoga mats; the kind I was convinced would have been utterly humiliating for me to have brought in. They walked into the room with the mat rolled up under their arm just as I had planned to do. A few people sat or lay on those mats, a few more sat on the meditation mat/cushion, but most of us just remained in our chairs as we were guided through the thought exercises.

In fact, Kristin Neff encouraged us to listen to our bodies and do what we felt most comfortable. I kept my chuckles to myself.

And I sat in my chair. I did put my computer down for the exercises and I survived the experience.

Self-compassion isn't selfish, but rather sets a person up to be much more able to open their heart to others in ways that are life giving to those around. When we are in a good place, we can be more fully present and compassionate to those around us. As a member of a family, or a local and world-wide community, it behooves us to be self-compassionate to be better able to connect with those around us.

Self-compassion makes for a better me. When I am a better me, I can be a better person to, and for, and in all my connections.

"Whenever I notice something about myself I don't like, or whenever something goes wrong in my life, I silently repeat the following phrases: This is a moment of suffering. Suffering is part of life. May I be kind to myself in this moment. May I give myself the compassion I need." **Kristin Neff**

I used to think that courage was about entering burning buildings or parachuting out of airplanes. Now I know that courage is also about whispering secrets in the dark and walking across the room for a conversation.

WIRED FOR CONNECTION

Fear is a part of courage

I used to think that courage was about entering burning buildings or parachuting out of airplanes. Now I know that courage is also about whispering secrets in the dark and walking across the room for a conversation.

THERAPY IS **NOT** FOR the faint of heart.

There is a cultural myth that weak, needy people go to therapy and that somehow, showing up at a therapist's office means you are one of those people.

The truth is this: the men and women who come into my office to work on the connections with themselves and others have a fierce courage that blows me away.

Continued suffering by pushing down, ignoring, and otherwise pretending that personal stuff isn't there is NOT the work of courage. When a person leans into the discomfort of facing whatever it is that creates internal distress—well, that **is** raw courage.

The vulnerability—the risk, uncertainty, and emotional exposure—that is required to walk into a therapist's room is enormous. A client who came to see me who was a therapist himself. As he sat down on the couch at the onset of his first session, he exclaimed, "Do you mean to tell me that my clients go through what I just did in the waiting room? I had no idea how nerve-wracking it is to wait to come into a session! I was freaking out in the waiting room!" We chuckled together at this awareness—at this very human emotion of fear as he felt the vulnerability of a first session as a client.

The courage I see in my counselling room in my clients has fundamentally changed my life. I ask questions of others that, when answered, will be sure to change their lives. They will reckon with pain and reality in fresh ways that cause irrevocable shifts. Those shifts are for healing and wholeness, to be sure—but require action and conversation.

- A man who recognizes for the first time that his wife's behavior isn't just nasty at times, it is abusive. For a man to acknowledge he is in an abusive marriage is a courageous acknowledgement indeed.

- An adolescent realizes she is feeling unloved and that she pulls for her caregivers to reject her by acting out and pushing people away. She is afraid to let anyone get close. She owns her "pushing away" behavior that results in the very distance she dreads. This is a courageous young woman.

- A woman realizes that the men around her get promoted ahead of her, even though she is just as capable. She begins to recognize in session that she unconsciously participates in a culture that

> makes her small. She avoids speaking up at meetings and doesn't apply for opportunities. The system is rigged against her, for sure—but she cooperates with the system. Gulp. This woman's picture is in the dictionary beside the word, "courage".

I have been wrecked by my clients' courage. If I am going to show up to meet with them again the following week after they have been so courageous—well, it means I have to be courageous in my own life.

I *had* to show up for TEDx because clients do terrifying things in their lives every week and I can't continue to work with them if I don't do the same. I had to continue weekly radio, even though fear hijacked me every time. (I promised myself I wouldn't quit until I stopped losing sleep the night before. It took about 20 months. Now I still do it—but I'm not losing sleep.) I needed to start the tough conversations with Jim, in our marriage, if clients left my office to go have hard conversations with their family. If I was going to continue working with courageous people with integrity, I needed to put on my own courage.

What is beautiful is that when I have chosen to engage in my life with courage—sometimes with gritted teeth, it has enriched my life immensely. It hasn't always gone swimmingly. At times, the results have been less than successful. However, overall, doing hard things has absolutely moved me forward.

Sometimes, to look my clients in the eye, I leap into the unknown with almost a resentment: "How dare you be so courageous with me and put me into this damn spot". And then later, gratitude: "I'm so glad your courage demanded mine—I did it!"

I have made friends, have deeper relationships, enjoyed bigger adventures, and discovered personal growth—all borne out of the courage I see in my clients. Simply, clients inspire me to be a more courageous person.

Sue and Joe have come to my office to discuss the latest argument. The arguments are getting more frequent and creating greater animosity that takes longer from which to recover. They seek to understand this argument so that they can stop what they fear is the slow, sinister slide towards divorce.

I start by asking about this latest argument. How did it begin?

Sue and Joe can't remember what started it. It lasted for days, hurt them both, but the origin of it is lost to both.

While that might sound odd, it's common. It's the same song, a different verse. Definitely the same chorus. The details vary, but the general pattern does not.

The argument began last week because of some infraction where he hadn't tidied something, polished it, made it symmetrical or cleaned it properly to her standards. This is the usual sort of onset.

She expressed her disappointment to him. He was silent.

She repeated herself to him because his lack of response might suggest he didn't hear it well.

Again, silence.

Now, she raises her voice to get through to him. She not only reiterates this present concern but reminds him of several past issues which he hadn't responded to at the time.

As she tells me how frustrating his silence is as she raises this issue in their original argument, I watch him in session. His arms are folded. His face was stony. His body stiff. Silent.

She begins crying. Something that is important to her is ignored by him and when she raises it, she experiences further lack of engagement. She looks at me in session and says: "See what I have to deal with? I'm trying to talk to him and he doesn't even care. He's doing it right now! Nothing."

I turn to Joe and gently say, "Sue is tearful because she thinks she doesn't matter to you. She sees that you aren't saying anything and to her, it means that you don't care."

He looks at me directly at me and, after a long moment, says quietly, "Of course I care. I don't even know how to show her how much I care. I guess I've kinda given up trying to show her how much I love her. Nothing I say or do will ever be good enough."

She looks at him and then at me impatiently. Sue gestures towards Ron and says: "He's just saying that now. If he really cared, he would talk to me when I come to him with a concern. He doesn't even know how to talk to me properly."

Joe looks at me, gives a vague shrug that says, "See?" and looks down.

I have a pulse oximeter on his finger that tells me, moment by moment, what his heart rate is. Joe is fit, average weight, with no health issues. He sits quietly, his pulse rate at 90.

Thirty or more beats above his resting heart rate.

It might look like he doesn't care on the outside. But on the inside, his body is keyed up.

I ask him if he can turn to her and say, "When I let you down, it feels like I'll only be good enough for you if I do everything to your standards. I'll never be able to do that and so I wonder if I can be enough for you."

He looks at me and says, "You want me to say that to her?"

And I ask, "Does it feel true to you?"

He nods and looks down. His pulse has just jumped to 110—while he is sitting perfectly still. He is terrified to turn to her to speak this out loud. He likes to leave and go quiet when he is uncomfortable. Now, I am asking him to stay and talk.

He swallows hard. He turns towards her slowly and clears his throat.

Then he says, "I forgot what you just said."

Fear does that, doesn't it? Makes us tongue-tied. Has us speak awkwardly and clumsily, or even incapable.

I remind him and his pulse remains high as he turns to her and haltingly says, "I love you so much and, in your eyes, I will always be a screwup to you. I don't know what to say when I just feel like a failure all the time." His eyes get a little moist, but he quickly clears his throat again to regain his composure.

I ask him: "What was that like to say to her?"

Bob: "Hard. But good, too."

I ask Sue: "What was that like to hear?"

Sue: "It's hard to wrap my head around it. I'm not any harder on him than I am on myself. I had no idea he felt like that." Her tone is hesitant, but softer now. She seems skeptical, but not closed to this revelation.

Bob's pulse has dropped back down to 90. Still high, but the fearful conversation he thought impossible has already created small change in their relationship.

The road back to each other has begun with a single step. An important one. They have discovered their courage to speak to each other with greater candidness. They need more conversation, but they have hope: a new relationship is possible.

For most of my life, I have used *courage* and *bravery* interchangeably.

When these concepts are swapped out for each other willy-nilly, it sets us all up to feel like cowards. When I do something I've never done before; something that feels frightening because it is fraught with risk, I get scared. So do you.

Our bodies use the feeling of fear as a signal to become apprehensive. The sweaty palms, racing heart, and nauseous feeling in our bellies tell us we are scared.

At that point, no matter whether we do the feared action or not, we are critical of ourselves because of the fear we feel. That sense of self judgement is hard. The fear is hard too.

The temptation is to move away from that which creates the fear to avoid the difficult feelings of fear and self-judgement altogether.

Some research I did for a workshop I delivered on courage recently taught me that these words are very d ifferent.[26]

Courage comes from the Latin word, *cor*, which means heart. Courage is about the thoughtful choice of measuring the risks and choosing to act, anyway. A feature of character, courage recognizes that there will be cost and proceeds to do the thing because the cost is worth it.

Courage, by definition, involves:

- feeling the fear,
- reeling from the risk,
- counting the cost

—and moving forward.

Bravery is different. Bravery comes from the Italian word, "*bravo*"—which is a big and loud word that is about boldness—but has flavours of savagery to it. It is gut instinct taking over to do something without considering the nuance of the action. It is jumping in with both feet on impulse.

Bravery is a quality that some people have more of than others. Jim is braver that I am when it comes to walking to the edge of a cliff and admiring the valley below. He laughs as I hold on to his shirt as I lean back behind him, determined to pull him back from certain death.

Have you ever seen an interview with a person who has just pulled a victim that was trapped in a burning car, or gone out onto thin ice to rescue someone who has fallen through into the freezing water? The interviewer says something like: "You're such a hero! You have so much courage! What you did put your own life at risk! "

The response is often something like, "Well, ummm—I don't think of myself as a hero. I just did what anybody would do. It was just instinct to go in and help. I didn't think about it."

That person was very brave in that moment. Not courageous. They didn't have time to notice the danger and feel the fear—they reacted instantly to save another. They won't notice their own bravery because fear never entered the equation.

We know it is courage when action is taken after internally processing all the factors involved in moving forward. A person sees the situation as intimidating and overwhelming, and they feel small and incapable of the task—and they still proceed.

This is a game changer! We only know an action as courageous when a person first acknowledged their uncertainty and fear. We don't do courageous things without fear, as bravery does.

By definition, courageous acts are only done while afraid.

If you're not scared, it's not courage.

It's as simple as that.

Here's an important idea if you connect the two ideas of what bravery is and what courage is together: doing something often enough in the spirit of courage builds bravery. One's capacity for risk increases with continued exercising of courage.

Jim, my husband, spent a summer as a young man working on apartment block construction as a framer. On his first day, it took an enormous amount of courage to be walking along 6-inch wide wooden beams when to fall down one side was an eight-foot drop and it was forty feet to the ground below on the other side. Over the courage of the summer, he became braver as he worked hour after hour up there carrying wooden boards to where they needed to go. The amount of courage required lessened, as there was less fear. His comfort level increased as his competence increased.

I see that as people practice courage in their own lives as they look to operationalize courage in their marriages, parenting, friendships, faith, and workplace. It takes a lot of courage to start open conversations about sexuality with your children, intimacy with your partner, or to speak up in a meeting when you are the junior person in the room.

It seems almost impossible the first time. The second time, still very hard. The third time, hard but do-able. Again and again. Rinse and repeat. An action that required enormous courage becomes part of your repertoire and now is a brave action because it doesn't involve fear.

We are quite familiar with the sort of courage that is required to accomplish amazing physical feats that involve heights, wild animals, fast or deep water, or extreme temperature. It obviously requires courage to climb a sheer mountain face hanging from hooks and rope, or to kayak white water rapids and the like.

What we don't always recognize is the courage required to:

- say, "I love you" first
- say, "I love you" for the first time in a long time
- apply for the promotion after not getting it last time
- making an appointment with the manager to find out why you didn't get the promotion
- seeing the lawyer to draw up a will

- talking to the doctor and asking all the questions about the suspicious lump
- asking someone out on a date after your divorce
- calling a friend when there is some vague Instagram post that indicates pain
- giving a performance review with critical feedback
- getting a performance review that contains critical feedback

We can avoid exercising courage by avoiding the fear every day. Or we can feel the fear, notice it, listen to it, and decide that to lean into the fear and do it anyway aligns with our values.

Courageous people choose to live on the edge of fear.

Bob and Sue will come to my office, and we will have a few occasions, each session, for them to turn to each other and name something out loud to each other that they can only say to me. Their pulse might race as they speak with courage, their voice may tremble, but they will open up to each other in a vulnerable way. They won't be running after each other or away from each other—rather, they will be leaning in towards each other. It will be uncomfortable, but they will be meaningfully connecting.

At the end of a session, I often ask clients which moments, from the session that is just ending, they will think about in the coming days. Not infrequently, they will discuss the moments where I had them turn to each other so one could courageously voice a truth that had never uttered before. Something so personal, so tender they could not whisper it out loud to the other before. And then they say something like, "And it didn't kill me. I'm still alive."

We laugh, in the way Anne Lamott speaks of as *carbonated holiness*. We come up for air as we recognize and honour the courage that was demonstrated in the room. There's a special sort of exhilaration present when, tenderly and carefully, people practice this quiet courage of allowing their tenderest selves to be deeply known.

It really does feel like one's life is on the line when practicing courage.

Our logical brains know that starting the conversation, walking into the manager's office, or making one's way onto the stage isn't life-threatening. But our racing mind and pounding hearts suggest otherwise in real ways.

We can spend our lives running away from all fear. Or we can lean in and make decisions about it in ways that change the trajectory of our lives.

A courageous life is lived by taking calculated risks. The courageous life embraces fear as an inevitable daily occurrence. By noticing the feeling of fear and using it as a cue to evaluate the danger, make plans to mitigate the danger, and then making a mindful choice considering that evaluation and planning to move forward, we move forward into living a life lived courageously.

"Courage is the most important of all the
virtues, because without courage you can't

practice any other virtue consistently. You can practice any virtue erratically, but nothing consistently without courage." Maya Angelou

I used to think that people who made bad choices were bad people. Now I know that we all try to solve our problems in ways that often create other problems.

WIRED FOR CONNECTION

Good people make wonky choices

I used to think that people who made bad choices were bad people. Now I know that we all try to solve our problems in ways that often create other problems.

SKIPPER WAS MY HUSBAND'S dog before I knew him. She was one of those large hunting-type dogs; an animal that can, and needs to, run for many miles. She was an odd choice of dog for a busy family to have as the family pet in the city, but they loved her. Although I never met her, I have heard stories about this much-loved pet.

Life at home was easier with Skipper after a good run that tired her out. She was happiest when she did what hunting dogs were born to do: run fast and far. Problem was, it wasn't easy to get her tired because her capacity for running was so large.

The family discovered that if they took her on a long run while they were riding their bicycle, Skipper could be in her glory. They would loop the handle of her leash over their handlebars, and the rider and Skipper would take off. She would run long and hard for miles. Then the family could relax, as Skipper would have a long happy snooze on her return.

There was an occasional, unexpected wrinkle to Skipper's run: Skipper **hated** lawnmowers.

It was not pretty.

Her hatred for lawnmowers was matched only by her hatred of toasters. (Burnt toast once led to a piercing smoke alarm which led to a lifelong fear of all things being toasted, but that's another story. But I apologize. I digress).

The cyclist and Skipper would ride and run for miles and then they would suddenly come across a person mowing their lawn—with a lawnmower—clearly, some sort of scary monster machine that had an engine that made noise and had obviously held some sort of imminent danger. And things would go sideways fast.

Skipper would PANIC!!

And when Skipper panicked, she did not run faster.

Oh no. No. Nope.

When Skipper panicked, she stopped cold.

Her leash was attached to the handlebars of the moving bicycle. Or, at least, the bicycle was moving until she stopped.

When the dog stopped, the bike, attached to the dog, also stopped.

The rider, not attached to the bike, **kept going**.

The bike crashed. The rider flew over the handlebars and landed hard. The bike would land on or near Skipper with a crash. In pain or surprise, often both, the rider would shout.

The rider would direct the energy of the shock and fall and pain towards the dog.

Picture this moment: both the new unceremoniously dismounted rider and Skipper had big feelings in that moment. Enormous feelings.

As the story is told by riders that had experienced this, Skipper would look up knowingly. She would peruse the bike on the ground, at the rider with the new bruises and scraped knee, and review the loud chaos that had just occurred.

Skipper would look at the rider, as if to say: "See! Now, do you understand why lawnmowers are scary? Lawnmowers are terrifying and you won't believe me!!"

None of us are immune to the inevitable travails of the reality of human existence:

- the furnace breaks down
- an elderly parent needs support during a move
- serious illness
- a lost job
- a child making devastating choices
- rent is due and there aren't funds to cover it

These aren't pleasant for certain. In fact, they can be very difficult. The big events of life can feel catastrophic.

The little events of life don't always feel little:

- when he leaves the glass on the counter AGAIN, instead of putting it in the dishwasher

- a flat tire when it is raining

- one of your employees doesn't get the information you need and now your boss is breathing down your neck

- it snows in April, and you need to shovel, AGAIN (This one might not make sense to you if you live in a warm climate, but trust me, a spring snow fall after a hard winter is distressing)

- the bus is full and goes right by your stop

A month later, you might forget any of these—but, at the moment, it feels BIG! Almost too much.

Things go wrong. They just do. Part of being alive is this: stuff happens. And, part of living as humans is that we have feelings—often big ones, that we may not recognize, or seek to avoid, or act out of without thinking—when challenges present themselves.

We influence situations—huge, monumental ones, as well as ones that felt monumental in the moment—by our own reactions. Others are influencing the same moment by their reaction—and we are further affected by what we experience as their responses.

I chuckle at the story of Skipper every time my family remembers it out loud. I believe I laugh at it because, far too often, I recognize my own reactions as they recount how Skipper creates her own dilemma and seemingly has no clue of it.

A *difficult situation* can develop into a *relationship or personal crisis* because of our own and others' response to the situation. We blame the situation, not realizing how the actions and reactions inflame the situation.

The situation snowballs. Fuel is added to the fire. Pick your metaphor.

If only we were a little more selective in picking our reaction.

Trying to put out a grease fire on a stove with water is not a good idea. Although it is instinct to put out fire with water—and in the kitchen, water is readily available—the water is a sure-fire way to have the fire explode in intensity. The water may not have created the fire, but it does create the disaster that follows. Go ahead, look it up on Youtube.

Good people have big feelings, and it shapes their reactions which then change the situation.

People armor up against their fear, shame, anxiety, or grief:

- A child complains about the supper meal you have prepared, and you snap back about starving children in Africa who would be grateful to have any food for supper. Shaming another person when we feel shamed is an automatic response for a lot of us.

- Your partner lets you know that to get to your destination, you should have taken a left-hand turn at the intersection you just passed. You remind your partner that they speed sometimes and they had an accident last year. Your voice is irritable and saucy—you have attitude. Fighting perceived criticism with criticism.

We avoid the pain, shame, fear of a situation by hiding, walking (or running) away:

- Your mother is critical (again) of how tight your clothes are, and you giggle. You make some casual comment about the lighting and change the subject—even though you're dying inside.

- Your spouse asks you to read a chapter of a book before having a conversation that connects the content of the chapter to your relationship. You agree to read the chapter "soon" and then announce that you need to go to the store to get a few groceries. No further mention of the chapter that evening or for days to come.

We can numb ourselves to avoid situations or feelings that seem too much, or too painful to handle:

- You're behind on the project, the boss gets on your case about it, and the day is so full of the requests of others that you never get to the project to catch up. You imagine the boss' reaction tomorrow and your stomach sinks. You go home and eat a carton of ice cream—and then a bag of potato chips. And then you feel sick.

- You look at the credit card bill and see how the amount due is larger than last month, and making only the minimal payment continues to worsen your overall financial health. It's hard to look at. To distract yourself, you go to the mall. While there, you find some really fine shoes that make you feel so much better when you try them on—and you purchase them on your credit card.

We may have any other number of responses that make some sort of life challenge worse:

- We hear such a fantastic story; we break a confidence in sharing a person's story to another

- You over share your own story with people who have not earned the right to hear it. There was a burning need to tell someone—but now you work with a colleague who knows more about you than appropriate.

- You give basic advice to someone in difficulty in ways that are experienced as insulting and minimizing. If something is that simple to resolve, the person would have come up with the easy stuff on their own. That person is now frosty towards you.

- You don't know what to do or say when someone shares something important. You are silent. No response at all. It's awkward. You might care on the inside, but there is no evidence to demonstrate this in your actions

People don't wake up in the morning determined to be a jerk. They just don't. They may have jerk-like behavior during the day, but they don't set out to be a pain/do evil/screw themselves or another person over. I have never known:

- an alcoholic who wakes up in the morning and says, "I want to wreck my life by drinking too much."

- A husband who says, "When I get home from work and my wife irritates me, I'm gonna ruin the evening by being twice the pain that she is."

- A mother who says, "When my children misbehave today, I'm going to destroy their sense of self-worth by calling them names."

I'm sure those people exist, but there aren't very many of them. Most of us wake up in the morning just wanting to make it through the day with mostly good stuff in it.

So many moments are so challenging in, well, the moment.

We look after the situation as best we can. I have found myself yelling at my children when they were small: "DON'T YELL!!" Even as I was engaging in this paradoxical act, I can't stop myself. I demonstrate the way to handle an overwhelming situation is to scream.

Behavior is better caught than taught, and I fear that my children caught lessons about how to handle difficult situations that I wouldn't have wanted them to absorb.

Maybe you can reflect on how you create a problem even as you seek to fix it:

- Your colleague continues to call you, "honey", even though you hate it. You say nothing, because you don't know what to say—but why would he change something he thinks you are fine with?

- During the pandemic, that one glass of wine before bed became two, and then you added a mid-afternoon happy hour glass as well. You didn't set out to have a drinking problem, but when your kids say you're often falling asleep on the couch and don't play with them like you used to, you know they are right. You intend to do better tomorrow, but those endless days of pandemic were so hard, you just went to the wine bottle in the same way the next day.

- Your spouse says you are unavailable and wants to spend more time with you working on the relationship. But you aren't quite sure what that means, and you don't know how to talk about it and it's uncomfortable and you get squirmy when this gets brought up. Work, however, is something you excel at. You know spreadsheets and formulas and your manager loves all the reports you send on time and in a very complete format. When you have an hour in the day, of course, you choose work and tell yourself that you are doing it to earn salary "for the family". We all default to spend time where we have competence.

And in our efforts to handle the situation, we react in ways that, in the moment are self-protective. They work—in the moment. In the big picture:

- they fray the relationship. Picture a very dull knife sawing on a thick rope—over months and years

- we lose credibility, sometimes in an almost imperceptible way in that single moment

- we self-sabotage: weight gain, alcoholism, loneliness, fatigue, debt, and the list goes on.

We notice later what we have done and we hate ourselves for it. Or we work hard to make sure we don't notice what we have done so we can't hate ourselves for it. Either of these are a problem, which—drum roll, please—we work to solve with a strategy that perpetuates the problem, or adds another.

These are Skipper moments. All of them.

I have a therapist colleague who often says, "We judge ourselves by our insides and judge others by their outsides."

People often have to think on that one for a bit.

There is a way in which we often are generous because we understand our own intentions and our own underlying good will. We do not understand other people's good intentions and the lens of shame often has people judge others and be suspicious. Generosity doesn't come naturally as we seek to protect ourselves from danger.

We often fail to give others the benefit of the doubt:

- When I am curt with my husband, I might know I have been too busy to eat so I am "hangry"—and I know that as soon as I sit down and have a meal and stop rushing, my mood will change. But, when he is curt with me (which happens rarely, the man has the patience of a saint), I immediately wonder why he has his shorts in a knot, how he could disrespect me like that, and wonder why he is so easily upset.

- When you give feedback in a job performance, you know that some of it was awkward and could have been said better—but you know that you did the best you could and giving critical feedback is hard and you haven't received enough training. When your manager gives you feedback in a job performance and some of it feels awkward and wasn't conveyed effectively, you decide that she is incompetent and mean. Maybe she's just a jerk.

This is a game changer: when others criticize, blow up, withdraw, or are irritable, angry, cynical, or any number of other reactions, it may well have more to do with them solving some internal problem than them lashing out or punishing you.

Wouldn't it be revolutionary to know that when someone relates to you poorly, it may well be their efforts to solve an internal problem with a strategy that actually creates another problem—for you personally, or between the two of you, as a couple?

Here's the deal: when someone is mean, or critical, or snide or sarcastic, it hurts—whether it is done intentionally or not.

When someone trips you and you land on your face, it hurts the same and your nose bleeds red whether the person intentionally stuck their foot out or didn't see you coming and inadvertently had their foot in the wrong place.

Your pain needs taking care of, regardless of the reason for the wounding. Full stop.

But motivation matters. You have the space to respond differently if the fall was inadvertent or unintentional.

If a hurt that comes to you is another person's effort to solve a problem by creating another problem, it opens the door for you to respond differently.

You still need to make decision to avoid continuing to put yourself in harm's way. But the other person is not labelled and dehumanized as a jerk. Rather, they are a hurt person who is hurting another person.

This creates a different sort of follow up conversation. Firm, clear, but kind and generous. The behavior played out to fix a problem and wasn't born out of spite or hatred. The behavior still needs to be addressed, but the conversation is completely different.

When:

- your colleague calls you "honey", you choose, with grace, to say, "I'm going to assume that 'honey' is said without awareness that it's not an appropriate name in the workplace. I'd feel more comfortable if you'd call me by my name."

- your partner walks in the door already irritable, you choose generosity to say, "I'm going to stay out of your way until you've cooled off from work. I think it's best to avoid giving you opportunity to say things that won't be good for either of us."

- Your partner promised to read a chapter, and two weeks later still hasn't, you try again, with compassion and clarity. "I've asked you to read 20 pages. I recognize this might be hard in a way that's difficult to identify. I know you love me, and part of loving me right now is following through on the chapter you told me you would read. Is there anything I can do to make it possible for you to get this done?"

Skipper didn't set out to harm the cyclist. It just happened as she reacted with fear to the lawnmower. She didn't intend for anyone to get hurt—and frankly didn't understand his role in the chaos and scraped knees that followed.

Skipper wasn't a "jerk" dog.

But the family did look at other ways for her to get the miles. While on the bike, they would listen carefully for potential lawnmowers in the distance and change their route. If they were approaching a lawnmower being used down the block, they had some choices—but they definitely knew to not to attempt to go full speed past the yard where the mower engine was revving.

"Good people will do good things, lots of them, because they are good people. They will do bad things because they are human." Harold S. Kushner

I used to think that tragedy was
always and inevitably all bad.
Now I know we can compost
awful experiences that can exploit
tragedy in life building ways.

Composting pain

I used to think that tragedy was always and inevitably *all* bad. Now I know we can compost awful experiences that can exploit tragedy in life building ways.

If you've experienced tragedy, you've likely heard the well-meaning but thoughtless platitudes people can say:

- Everything happens for a reason
- There is a purpose for this—look for it. You'll come out richer and stronger for this.
- What doesn't kill you makes you stronger (Thank you, Kelly Clarkson!)

In other words, celebrate that you have just experienced unspeakable pain, because it will be worth it in the end.

Hearing these lines amid pain can have a person want to vomit a little in their mouth—or restrain themselves from violence on the person saying such things. On an occasion such as this, it might feel good to punch someone in the nose. (I trust most people don't follow through on their swing, but I talk to people who can feel their hands ball up into fists.)

I believe people say such things during times of tragedy because they don't know what the right thing is to say. They want to make it better. (Hint: there is no fixing the big feelings of grief and sadness that come with painful experiences by trying to make the big feelings smaller. There is no *jollying up* pain.)

There is a human impulse to make the pain of others *less worse*—because it is so darn uncomfortable watching someone else hurt. And so, the outcome is well-intentioned but stupid sentences.

Anyone who has experienced the death of a loved one, or suffered the death of a lifelong dream, or received catastrophic news about their own health—there is no *making it better.*

No growth, however substantial and beautiful will make tragedy *worthwhile*. It just doesn't.

There is no *silver lining* to your spouse dropping dead, getting fired for being the whistleblower, or watching your child lose their battle to cancer. Full stop.

Pain hurts. It just does.

While I don't wish pain on anybody, I do wish for people to exploit their inevitable pain for good.

I revel in **redemption**—turning the pain of life into something that is good for me or for others.

My clients have taught me, again and again, that while they didn't wish for or ask for tragedy, when they find ways to exploit the pain of tragedy, the world—and they—become richer for it.

And I am here for being richer.

If we can turn the non-optional pain into good—let's do it!

I consider this *emotional composting.*

Turning the eggshells, vegetable peelings, and other organic crap into fertile soil is all about turning that which we cannot use and does not serve a useful purpose into a rich compost that will create nutrients for future growth.

When we find ways of composting our pain, we grow, and those around us grow.

I don't wish for the pain—but pain is an inevitable part of being alive. And if the pain is coming anyway, then using it to make the world a better place seems to be a way to beat tragedy at its own game.

A few years ago, my husband, Jim, and I were part of an article[27] in the Globe and Mail, a national daily newspaper in Canada. Zosia Bielski, a writer from the Globe, contacted me after reading about our story at the Conexus Counselling blog[28]. I had written about our story on the counselling website. Zosia wanted to write about finding love soon after losing a spouse in a style that was compassionate and understanding.

I emailed her, letting her know that the topic of finding love after recently losing a spouse was something I had much more than a professional opinion on.

Finding love *quickly* after a spouse dies is a deeply personal topic for me.

I have written often and easily about my relationship with my husband, whom, publicly, I refer to as "Husband". Jim is wonderful in a multitude of ways. Writing about his compassionate and kind nature comes easily to me. But I am quite a private person and protective of my family—I write about characteristics, qualities, and dynamics of my family to illustrate concepts and thoughts but always without specific names and identifying details.

Now Zosia was asking me what my husband's name was to print in an article. Even more, early in the interview, she asked me exactly how much time passed between his first wife, Car's death, and our marriage.

I've never put that fact in my writing on the website. Maybe I didn't want everyone to know how brief a time it was. Maybe I didn't want to open myself up to ridicule and judgement.

Ok, cancel the "maybe". That was it. I didn't want people to know the truth.

And now, she was asking for it, so it could be published online for the entire country to see. Jim and I became engaged 11 months after his beloved wife died and married 2 months later. Thirteen months after his wife died, we got married. When that article would be published, the entire country would know—and could judge us.

Gulp.

I had a conversation a while back with a coach of a national level team that was ranked Number 1 in the country. The team was racking up enormous numbers of wins and was heading towards another championship. They had won the national trophy the year before and were hurtling towards another victory.

He was my son's coach, and he was at my house for a pregame dinner, along with the rest of the team. To engage in interesting conversation, I asked him about the season thus far, and how he felt going into the second half of the season. I wondered about his perceptions of the chances that the team would bring all that championship hardware home.

He told me something interesting. The coach said that he knew his team was excelling, but he wasn't sure that they had what it took to take them down the home stretch.

Coach had concern the team hadn't had to face enough adversity that year.

He reflected on other years, where there had been significant challenges with injuries or other difficulties. In his mind, facing challenges together creates growth, and enhances a sense of "team". Overcoming difficulties is one way a team gels, which enhances performance. He felt difficult challenges gave the team a competitive edge they couldn't otherwise achieve.

For the purposes of creating a successful team, he knew struggling together was essential.

It is something I've mulled about since: A coach appreciating the fruit of a team struggling with hardship.

He believed the alchemy of tribulation was important to the team's success.

This coach was a kind man and wouldn't wish for any athlete on his team to have back surgery, or be out with a badly sprained ankle, or struggle with family issues that created huge mental health challenges. He wouldn't want it to happen—but he was aware of the reality that these sorts of adverse experiences developed strength and resilience. As the team surrounded a struggling athlete, they became a more cohesive group that knew how to do hard things—together.

The smooth path towards victory continued through the remaining months of the season.

The team was heavily favoured to win because everything was looking positive.

They lost in the finals that year.

As Zosia was writing this article, it seemed she was already imagining the layout, including visuals. And she felt a picture of Jim and me would be helpful. She asked for one.

It was easy to buy myself some time. I couldn't say yes to her without Jim also agreeing, of course. I said I'd talk to him and get back to her.

It was also a needed opportunity to create space for me to decide if I wanted our picture published in a national newspaper by a writer with whom I'd only had a brief phone conversation.

Jim got home a few hours later, and I asked him what he thought. He asked me what I thought before he answered–that's how we roll. We talked about the vulnerability of sending a picture to be used in an article about how harshly people can judge. The truth was that judgement was the automatic response that the author was trying to write people out of—if she was successful. Total strangers who looked at only the facts could be mean. It seemed like we were setting ourselves up for being skewered by criticism.

Vulnerable, for sure.

But we asked ourselves:

"What if some good could come out of this pain?"

One of my favorite shows, *This is Us*, has a line of dialogue that appeared in the first show and is then threaded throughout the series beautifully:

> "Sometimes life is about taking the sourest lemons that life has to offer and making something resembling lemonade."
>
> Dr. Katowski, This is Us

In the initial episode, the obstetrician says this line to Jack, as Jack absorbs the reality that one of his children died in childbirth, and the physician invites him to take home another infant just dropped off at a nearby fire station. It seems too big an ask at such a moment of pain. Jack looks at him, uncomprehendingly.

I like the idea of turning the pain of our lives into something that is palatable—even delicious. Part of the best glass of lemonade is the cheek-puckering sour taste of the lemons. Turning something that is painful crap into something good—composting.

Going through painful life experiences *hurts like heck.*

Why wouldn't we want to use every opportunity to turn the painful crap of our lives into something resembling rich compost? Compost provides a nutrient rich medium that enhances growth.

We can't undo the hurt. We can't stop painful and unfair experiences in lives. But we can compost the heartbreak. We can make it into something that doesn't have to stay ugly and soul destroying—it becomes life giving and redemptive.

Turning the pain into something life-giving just seems redemptive.

I have two values I lean into—as I decide how to dedicate my energy and focus my life, I measure it up against these two values.

The first is reflected in the name of my company, and the title of this book: ***connection***. I'm all about enhancing relationships—my own and to help others with theirs.

The second value that I live by is: ***redemption***.

When I was in my 20s, my first pregnancy ended in stillborn twins. The one time in my life when I literally feared losing my mind was in grief after their death. I was gutted. The physical pain of grief made it hard to breathe. I was exhausted and lost. It was, without a doubt, the most painful experience of my life.

There are reminders of Branden and Matthew in most rooms of my home. I still miss them, and every fibre of my being wishes they were alive, and I had spent all these years knowing them, loving them, raising them.

I *so wish* they hadn't died.

But I will also tell you that when I see clients after a loss, I can identify with them. When people feel lost in grief, I am more compassionate and understanding. I know that experiencing the deaths of my children changed me in fundamental ways.

I believe the loss of these little guys has made me a much better therapist. There are people who have gotten better therapy from me because I'm wiser, more thoughtful, more tender than I would be without that experience.

I love the idea of redemption of the inevitable painful and ugly of our lives.[29]

The picture we sent Zosia was this one:

photo credit: Denley Thiessen

It's our favorite wedding picture. We made a large image of this on canvas and have it hanging in our room. I love it.

My favourite part of this picture is what you don't see. Can't see.

You see, it was a sunny day in April when we posed for these. Apparently, the photographer didn't think the lighting was right.

So, he asked our kids to make us shade.

This is another angle of the same pose, taken moments after the above snap:

photo credit: Denley Thiessen

This is us.

And this is all of us, for real. This is one of my favourite memories of the day. These crazy, fun-loving kids, full of antics. They showed up to enjoy the day. We laughed as they sought to create as broad a shade as humanly possible. They worked together as a team—his sons and mine—along with a couple extra that have since become our daughters-in-law.

The wedding that day was only because of devastating loss—the end of the marriages of their biological parents. This is not something they ever had wanted. The wedding day must have been a hard day in some ways for them, even as they ate yummy cupcakes and played basketball with their buddies.

We invited their friends, and they all brought their gym shorts and they had a blast that day. But it was only possible because of the heartbreak—the end of the marriage of their parents.

The picture we sent the journalist is a beautiful picture–and an even better memory. When I look at the picture, I can hear the playful banter as they jostled to figure out how much shade they could make as they worked together.

We do better under the shade of those who love us.

People create a gentle shade when they are gentle and loving and caring. *They get it* because tragedy has softened some of their hard edges, and they understand the depth of suffering of others.

On our wedding day, the metaphor of their shade for us was powerful. As parents, we sought to be there for them, support them, help them, and give them a space to escape the worst harshness that life offers. Now they were hovering around and above us, giving us what we needed as we celebrated our love amid a wild, hurtful, and exquisite life. They worked together as a team that day in a way we would not have dared expect.

We get through the hard times and turn that heartbreak into beautiful compost when we have the support and love of those who are in our lives. Don't we all need people to cheer us on and shield us when the harsh light of our lives gets to be too much? We can't stop the hard things happening to the people who love us, but we can sit with them in it—and that, people tell me, makes a difference.

Love and heartbreak recover best and turn into the most beautiful compost under the conditions of love, laughter, and support.

We are in this painful, beautiful journey together—composting heartbreak.

"I know now that we never get over great losses; we absorb them, and they carve us into different, often kinder, creatures." **Gail Caldwell**

Afterword

I started this book during the pandemic. It took me many months to write, and many more months to edit—and I've been discouraged. Writing is solitary—and so sitting hour after hour in front of the computer has been impossible. The pandemic affected a lot of us—and continues to impact us—sometimes in ways that we wouldn't suspect. The line isn't always as straight and obvious as we would like—but the three years of altered rhythms to our relationships had a cost to our souls. We are wired for connection—first to ourselves and then to others. We all experienced disruptions in our wiring that has ongoing impacts.

You have, in your hands, the first of 3 volumes of Wired for Connection—relationship lessons that clients taught a therapist. This comes with the support and care of my community and family. I'm looking forward to sharing more.

By now, you might have guessed that as I'm writing about the lessons my clients taught me, I do it just as much for myself as for you. I reflect and write these ideas, and in so doing, consolidate and further imprint these ideas in my head, and belief of them in my spirit.

A huge thanks for spending your most valuable asset, your time, with this book. You have chosen to connect with this book—and with me—and I am grateful. I'd welcome your suggestions, edit suggestions, or requests for speaking to contact@carolynklassen.com

Please leave a five-star review if you liked this book. I'd be most grateful.

1. Anderson, Chris. Ted Talks: The Official Ted Guide to Public Speaking. Published by Collins, an Imprint of HarperCollins Publishers Ltd, 2017.
   This book is excellent in skill building, but also heart and soul building for the person who is a tentative public speaker.

2. Anderson, Chris. page 4.

3. Anderson, page 184. Seriously, this is a great book to understand that public speaking is challenging for our spirits.

4. "Learning From the Sequoias: The Value of Interconnectedness | Carolyn Klassen | TEDxWpg." YouTube, 2 Oct. 2018, www.youtube.com/watch?v=S9BJjkijb2I.

5. Holt-Lunstad, Julianne. 2021. "Julianne Holt-Lunstad: Is Social Disconnection Comparable to Smoking? | TED Talk." TED: Ideas Worth Spreading. May 4, 2021. https://www.ted.com/talks/julianne_holt_lunstad_is_social_disconnection_comparable_to_smoking.

6. (Holt-Lunstad 2021)

7. Waldinger, Robert, and Marc Schulz. 2023. The Good Life. Simon and Schuster.

8. Waldinger, Robert. 2015. "Robert Waldinger: What Makes a Good Life? Lessons from the Longest Study on Happiness | TED Talk." TED: Ideas Worth Spreading. December 23, 2015.
   https://www.ted.com/talks/robert_waldinger_what_makes_a_good_life_lessons_from_the_longest_study_on_happiness/transcript?language=en.

9. Hari, Johann. 2019. Overcoming Addiction in Canada by Building Recovery Capital and Building on Our Strengths. Winnipeg: Recovery Capital Conference.

10. Haidt, Jonathan. 2021. "This Is Our Chance to Pull Teenagers Out of the Smartphone Trap." The New York Times, July 31, 2021.

11. Twenge, Jean M. 2017. "Have Smartphones Destroyed a Generation? - The Atlantic." The Atlantic. https://www.facebook.com/TheAtlantic/. August 3, 2017. https://www.theatlantic.com/magazine/archive/2017/09/has-the-smartphone-destroyed-a-generation/534198/.

12. Taylor, Jill Bolte. 2008. My Stroke of Insight. Penguin.

13. Brackett, Marc. 2019. Permission to Feel. Celadon Books.
This is a stellar book to recognize the impact of emotion on our lives, and then provides the reader with skill development strategies to improve emotional literacy.

14. Brown, Brené. 2021. Atlas of the Heart. Random House. p. xxi

15. Here are a few books to get you started with developing emotional literacy:
Brackett, Marc. 2019. Permission to Feel. Celadon Books.

Brené Brown. 2021. Atlas of the Heart. Random House.

and yes, there's an app for that!
Mood Meter: https://www.marcbrackett.com/about/mood-meter-app/

16. Bergen, Carolyn. 2010. "Authenticity Trumps Perfection - Conexus Counselling - Winnipeg Manitoba." Conexus Counselling. https://www.facebook.com/BergenandAssociatesCounselling/?fref=ts. October 22, 2010. https://conexuscounselling.ca/2010/10/22/authenticity-trumps-perfection/.

17. Brown, Brené. 2010. "Brené Brown: The Power of Vulnerability | TED Talk." TED: Ideas Worth Spreading. December 23, 2010. https://www.ted.com/talks/brene_brown_the_power_of_vulnerability.

18. Brown, Brené. 2015. Daring Greatly. Penguin. p. 69

19. Brown, Brené. 2015. Daring Greatly. Penguin. p. 68. This book is a game changer, really. A lot of people start with this book when they are trying to understand their inner world and how shame changes it.

20. Brown, Brené. 2017. Rising Strong. Random House. p. 84.
This book is great to have you think through your stories allowing you to be the author of your story. Another great book that I love to invites the reader to think through their life as a story is:
Miller, Donald. 2009. A Million Miles in a Thousand Years. Thomas Nelson.

21. Again, from Rising Strong by Brené Brown. Page 81.

22. Brown, Brene. 2017. "The Swim of Awakening with Brené Brown | Spirituality+Health." Spirituality+Health. July 23, 2017. https://www.spiritualityhealth.com/articles/2017/07/23/the-swim-of-awakening-with-bren%C3%A9-brown.

23. Neff, Kristin. 2011. Self-Compassion. Harper Collins.

24. Talks, TEDx. 2013. "The Space Between Self-Esteem and Self Compassion: Kristin Neff at TEDxCentennial-ParkWomen." YouTube. February 7, 2013. https://www.youtube.com/watch?v=IvtZBUSplr4.

25. Neff, Kristin. n.d. "Definition and Three Elements of Self Compassion | Kristin Neff." Self-Compassion. https://www.facebook.com/selfcompassion. Accessed July 18, 2023. https://self-compassion.org/the-three-elements-of-self-compassion-2/.

26. Waters, Shonna, 2021. "Bravery versus Courage: What is the Difference?" The Most Comprehensive Coaching Platform, BetterUp, July 1, 2021 https://www.betterup.com/blog/bravery-vs-courage#:~:text=Now%20you%20know%20the%20key,times%20when%20they're%20appropriate.

27. Bielski, Zosia. 2018. "Too Soon? Why We Harshly Judge the Widowed When They Find New Love - The Globe and Mail." The Globe and Mail. The Globe and Mail. January 15, 2018. https://www.theglobeandmail.com/life/relationships/too-soon-why-we-harshly-judge-the-widowed-when-they-find-newlove/article37607669/.

28. Bergen, Carolyn. 2015. "Visiting My Husband's Wife's Grave - Conexus Counselling - Winnipeg Manitoba." Conexus Counselling. https://www.facebook.com/BergenandAssociatesCounselling/?fref=ts. October 9, 2015. https://conexuscounselling.ca/2015/10/09/visiting-my-husbands-wifes-grave/. (Note: My name before I married Jim was Carolyn Bergen. I changed it to Carolyn Klassen and my website was slow to catch up!)

29. Bergen, Carolyn. 2014. "Redemptive Suffering - Conexus Counselling - Winnipeg Manitoba." Conexus Counselling. https://www.facebook.com/BergenandAssociatesCounselling/?fref=ts. November 1, 2014. https://conexuscounselling.ca/2014/11/01/redemptive-suffering/.

About the Author

Carolyn Klassen has completed a Master of Arts degree in Marriage, Family, and Child Counselling in Fresno, California. She also has a degree in Occupational Therapy from the University of Manitoba and then taught for many years in this program..

Carolyn Klassen is a therapist in Winnipeg, and speaker at Wired for Connection. A Certified Daring Way Facilitator, she believes that fundamentally, all of us are wired for connection, and that meaningful relationships have tremendous healing power. Her many years of providing therapy provide her with a wealth of knowledge about people—including topics like grief, pain, anxiety, depression, joy and grace that are not easily or often spoken about in polite company. Her presentations and writing are interesting, laced with story, rooted in scientific research while being real and profoundly human.

Carolyn is an author, is a regular contributor to 680 CJOB "Connecting Winnipeg" show with Hal Anderson and frequently appears on news programs as an expert on relationships and mental health.

She loves lattés, family suppers, busy bird feeders, sun porches, and reading books endlessly to her grandchildren.

Also By Carolyn Klassen

Nice to a Fault: Redefining Kindness in Marriage
Is there still time to run? A message from your therapist before your first session
Thinking Therapy—From No to Maybe: Making a wise and thoughtful decision about therapy

Made in the USA
Middletown, DE
10 May 2024

54143010R00096